Anne Liberty

Sashiko

for Beginners

and

Sashiko

Projects

A Simple Guide to Learn the Japanese Quilting, Embroidery and Stitching

Table of Contents

Introduction

Sashiko is a traditional Japanese embroidery technique that uses straight stitching to create a textured pattern on fabric. The word Sashiko is a combination of the words sashi (needle) and koso (to sew), and it originated in the 9th century. It's used for decorative stitching in textiles, garments, bags, and much more.

Sashiko is a very simple form of Japanese embroidery that originated in the mid-1700s as part of a peasant revolt.It has been used to decorate items ranging from miniature flags to backpacks and even T-shirts.

Sashiko stitching can be done on anything, as long as it is flat and fairly thick. We've seen it done on boxes, tablecloths, blankets, towels, household goods, and industrial items. It is only limited by what you can find to use as a base material. Sashiko is the ideal stitch for those who don't want to use pre-made patterns, but still want something neat and decorative on their knitted or crocheted project.

In this book, we will give some fundamental strategies utilized in Sashiko embroidery and offer some valuable tips for making basic and a la mode plans. While it might look muddled, Sashiko is really simple to learn and enjoyable to ace.

Since it is only an assortment of straightforward running fastens, this strategy is to some degree like sewing by hand. So I trust that this book will assist you with getting a vibe of how to manage various types of examples and acquaint you with the superb universe of Sashiko!

Getting Started in Sashiko

Over the years, Sashiko evolved, beating every odds and is in full use today. The major application of this form of embroidery is decorative purposes; giving and improving aesthetic value of clothes, handbags, tapestries, tableware's and all. No doubt, this traditional Sashiko style has come to be appreciated by all.

Getting started in Sashiko, however, doesn't come with laid down rules for you to follow. The kind of fabric and color of yarn to use solely depends on how you want your Sashiko to look like. Well, you can apply the right techniques due to accumulated experience. On progressing, there's need to create an area or territory, mapped out specifically for weaving, and these are popularly known as patterns. Patterns can come pre-printed with lots and lots of options to choose from. However, one must be careful as they come with both benefits and disadvantages.

Thread choice is solely dependent on you. The thread used for regular weaving, the traditional kind, have soft twist, giving it an easy feel to work with. You can find these threads in various colors. They are seen with skeins and undergo some forms of preparations before stitching.

You'll need suitable needles to go along with the threads. Sashiko needles have become much popular and a household item for those involved in the embroidery craft. When compared with other weaving needles, they are much longer and also can accommodate stitches, during weaving, before a final pull of fabric. Friction between fabric and needle can cause fraying in threads. The long length of Sashiko needles helps in reducing this.

Mapping out your patterns can be done either by drawing directly on the fabric or transferring the design through a medium, to the fabric. The goal is to make sure that the pattern comes out clean and clear as the complexities of stitching may cause the pattern to wear off. You don't have a need to worry if your pattern is well visible, the outcome will be good.

You can start with selecting a good fabric for your Sashiko embroidery. One of such specialty common then was the indigo-dyed hemp fabric. You can find this in some special art and crafts shops. The fabrics in vogue are usually the loosely woven cotton of medium weight, linen or the cotton and linen blend of fabric. Also, on selecting a good fabric, the weaving technique is one aspect to consider. Working with cotton fabric with thick threads and heavy needles as cotton itself are tightly woven, especially the batiks. The stitching process can be seen to create holes and puckering. Pre-washing your fabric is a good way to start. You can totally eliminate the possibility of dye transfer which can greatly affect your work.

After choosing the particular fabric for your Sashiko, next up is to prepare the pattern. The normal thing one would have done is to cut the pattern or design to be used, out, but in this case only tracing of pattern is needed. With a ruler, create lines for actual stitching. This will go a long way in preventing you from tampering with seam allowance. Some designs can be curvy-like and this can depend on use of grid system. The grid technique is usually done by those with a good level of experience and what they do is, drawing a grid on the fabric and creating the pattern directly, and in the process, stitching the corners. Well, working with patterns is usually our thing, so, you can choose varieties of them from different sources or create them yourself.

Making your fabric comes next. One tool suitable for this method is the Hera Marker which is invasive minimally. It comes with the advantage of not having to refill or sharpen. You're always on the move with this. How this works is by applying pressure on the edge of the tool and then, create drawings on the fabric. The creased lines made by these, provides an avenue for stitching.

Go ahead and transfer the pattern. There are several tools you can try. The chalk paper, tailor's carbon paper, tracing tool, tissue paper, transfer pen, light box, name it. On trying to use the chalk paper or carbon paper, place the fabric on a level surface and support with weight or tapes to prevent it from slipping off. On the fabric, spread the paper, chalk face down, then place the pattern on and trace out the outline using a pointed object or tracing tool. Placing a plastic cover over pattern while tracing can smoothen the process but, it is not all that necessary.

Brief History

Sashiko is known to have originated from Japan's rural north and spread to the South along trade routes. Sashiko's specific origins have been lost to time and it is believed to have probably developed during the Edo period (1615-1868). This Edo period was a time when Japan closed her borders to foreign travel, trade and ideas. The laws for Japanese citizens were repressive and detailed and there were some that forbade commoners from wearing silk, bright colors and large designs. These laws were called sumptuary laws and we're designed to keep the class lines clear. Sashiko became well established in the Meiji era.

Japan has a lot of beautiful fabrics but the Sashiko is unique and is referred to as a "folk textile" because it was predominantly made and used by the peasant classes. The women from farming and fishing families made Sashiko mostly during the winter period. The lifespan of fabrics were extended with Sashiko and it helped reduce the cost of the families.

Fabric production was done locally and traditionally in Japan for a very long period as industrialized production of fabric did not start in Japan until the 1870s. When mechanized Mills were finally built in Osaka, the fabrics were too costly for many people. This therefore encouraged most people to continue to weave their own fabric for clothing and household items. This was even worse in northern Japan because cotton could not grow due to the fact that the weather was too cold.

Mending of clothes was essential for survival and Sashiko was a major part of a mending technique called 'boro'. Boro is translated in Japanese to mean "tattered rags". Boro textiles have multiple shades of indigo fabric that are patched or quilted together in a neat way with Sashiko stitches, helping to cover holes and reinforce worn areas.

Worn out garments were quilted into work wear using the Boro technique and this served to increase the lifespan of clothes and household textiles. The clothing's always came out warmer and stronger as the women would quilt two or three layers together, putting the oldest cloth in the middle, where it could still be useful, but hidden. Sometimes, even the worn out work wear where made into bags and aprons and the fabrics from these items could then be quilted one last time into thick cleaning clothes.

Sashiko Tools and Materials

Before you can start embroidery, you have to be acquainted with a few things. That's some knowledge on how to embroider, a good pattern to make your project unique, and above all the tools and materials you need to create your first ever decorative stitches. The tools and materials will be explained below.

Embroidery Needles

Embroidery needles come with a medium length, long eye, and sharp point. They are found in sizes 1 to 12, among the sizes, 1 is the largest while 12 is the smallest. It is good for general embroidery and most especially for beginners.

Embroidery Floss

Embroidery Floss also knew as stranded cotton is very popular with a rainbow of colors. It contains six separate plies that can be kept apart or joined to achieve a thickness that is best for your project.

Embroidery Hoops

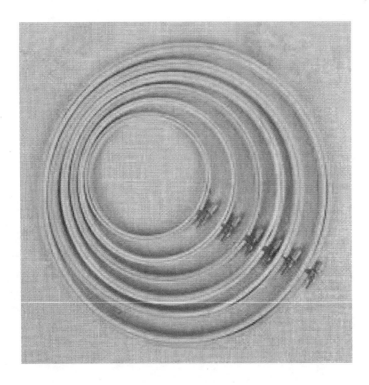

When I'm stitching, I used an embroidery hoop to hold my fabric taut and firmly in position as I go stitching, this gives way for even stitching and avoids squeezing or folding. There are so many sizes of hoops, which are indicated by their diameters in inches.

As for my project, I chose one that surrounds the whole design. If you wish to place the fabric into the hoop, ease the joining screw and set apart the two rings; while you layer the fabric over the inside ring and press hard on the outside ring down within the inside ring; cock the screw again, and this safeguard your fabric in the embroidery hoop.

Novelty Embroidery Floss

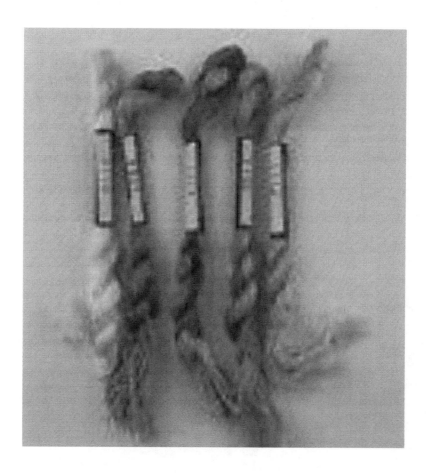

Apart from the basic embroidery floss and pearl cotton, there is a whole lot of assorted specialty fibers that are available in the market: multiple-colored matte thread, glittered thread, even glow-in-the-dark thread-often as a polyester.

You are free to explore, but you have to remember to pair your thread with the appropriate needle size. Scissors:

There is a whole lot of scissors you will be needing during your embroidery to help you perform certain tasks.

Some types of embroidery scissors are very small in size having a sharp point, which makes them excellent for snipping threads and taking away undesired stitches. Whereas fabric shears are great for cutting fabrics.

There are some scissors referred to as all-purpose scissors; they are good for cutting out patterns especially on transfer paper.

Pear Cotton

Pear Cotton not be divided; hence they are made of twisted strands. It is usually in both skeins and spools. Due to its line stitches, a heavier textured feel - such as the chain stitch or stem stitch - sits high up on the fabric, which makes it a great choice for surface embroidery.

Felt

Felt contains texture and thickness which sticks well to embroidered stitches. It will not unravel at the edges. You can find it in natural wool also, even in synthetic fibers such as across or rayon.

Sashiko Needles

Sashiko Needles are long, sturdy, and particularly made for the running stitch.

In other words, it is designed in such a way that it enables you to load multiple stitches onto it before pulling it through the fabric. They are of different sizes according to their type; traditional ones are about 2 inches while making modern ones are shorter and have a larger eye for smooth threading.

Silk Thread

Silk thread is a very vital material for embroidery, it is fine and soft. Among all-natural fibers, silk is the strongest, and also has the highest sheen. The greatest importance of working with silk is that it doesn't create holes, dyes very well, and it is of two forms viz: filament with a single strand or spun with heavier strands.

Wool Yarn

This is a natural fiber which last-longer, with colorfast, and wears well for many years. For embroidery Sach, the thread is classified under 3 main varieties viz: fine crewel yarn, divisible 3-ply Persian wool, and tapestry wool.

Ribbon

The ribbon is often used in ribbon embroidery, adds bright luster and dimension to floral designs, romantic vignettes, and more. Among the ribbons, my preferred materials are satin and silk, because it moves smoothly with every stitch of the hand.

Bending Needles

Bending needles comes with an added small eye and flexible, long shaft. They mostly come in different sizes of 10 to 15, with 10 as the largest and 15 the smallest. Because of their fine size and flexibility, they are the greatest choice for threading seed beads and other tiny holes.

Over-Dyed Thread

According to its name, "over-dyed" non-divisible thread comes with many colors that harmoniously progress from one to the other. This is differentiated from variegated thread or floss, which comes with complicated shades of a single color.

Quilting Needles

Quilting needles consist of a small, roundish eye and a short shaft. They are of different sizes of 3 to 12, with 3 as the largest and 12 the smallest. They're the best needle for traditional hand quilting due to their ability to permit quick, precise stitches between layers of fabric.

Sashiko Stitching Tips and Techniques

This chapter discussed the tips and techniques you will need as you go on with various projects.

How to Prepare Sashiko Thread?

1. Open the skin and take away the paper band.

2. Look for the added loop within the skin and cut through all threads at this point.

3. Cut the other/opposite end of the loop.

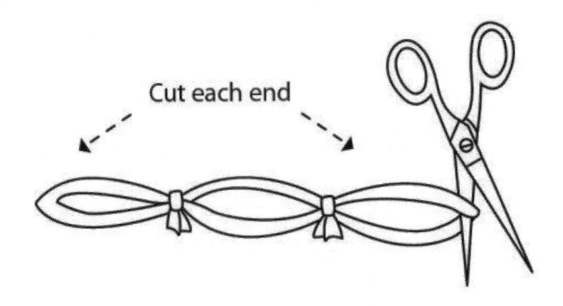

Cut each end

Bundles of thread have to separate into two. Turnover one of the two bundles of thread at 180°. Sashiko threads have a twist and this will enable the twist to go through the same way throughout the bundle.

Grip the whole bundle and remove one thread, cut it into three pieces, and tie the bundle in three places firmly with a squared knot. For Sashiko thread use lengths not longer than 20-24" long, this is because Sashiko threads tend to fray.

Tips

The thread works better when threaded so that you could pull with the twist rather than against it like you on stitching. If you want to test the twist, grip up one particular thread and pinch close to the top of the thread between your thumb and forefinger and run your fingers down the through the length of the thread.

One way will be rough while the other way will be smooth. Tie a colored thread at the top of the tip of the thread bundle that feels smooth as you run your fingers down it. It is at this end you will always pull your thread and thread your needles.

Pass your Sashiko thread through beeswax or a silicone thread conditioner. The Sashiko thread will move softly and smoothly through the cloth and there will be little chance of it separating.

How to Stitch a Sashiko Design?

1. Remove one thread from your traditional Sashiko bundle, thread it through the large eye of the shape needle, and tie one knot at the end.

2. Raise the threaded needle from the back of the marked fabric background. Stitching may begin at any spot along with the design, but be careful because it will not require too many twists, turns, or long spaces on the back.

3. The point of the needle should be placed flat on the design line a little distance away from the point at which the thread springs up, and measure. With this, it will help you to determine how long the stitches should be before you pull it through the fabric.

If the needle is held straight up before taking a stitch, the point may not balance on the line or you may wrongly judge the length of the stitch.

Tips

In Japanese sewing, the needle is held straight and the fabric is positioned on it in a pleating move. You have to place light tension on the fabric and rock it, as you collect various stitches onto the needle. Traditionally, the top stitch is slightly longer than space in between. But not that, uniformity is far better than stitch length.

Pull the needle and thread through to the knot. Take 2-3 stitches onto the needle. Maintain the same length for the stitch, about 5-7 inches for each inch.

After the stitching of one or two inches, take up on the thread a little; then, with your thumb, gently, extend out the stitching. The point here is to keep the work loose, mostly the thread on the back, so that the stitching doesn't squeeze.

Traditional Sashiko

In traditional Sashiko, instructions are provided detailing the directions in regards to the stitching routes to take and the number of stitches to perform for each leg of the design, but as you gather more confidence and experience, you will now develop your own methods and patterns.

The point is to keep the stitches even and maintaining smooth lines.

Tips:

A stitch must end at the turn of a corner, either moving up to the top of the thread going to the back. To stitch closed curves, reduce the stitches a little.

Those threads that skip across the back should not be longer than half an inch. Loosen the strand on the back to prevent squeezing. Most times, a longer skip can be prevented by weaving the thread across various stitches on the back to reach a new section of the marked design.

Finishing a Line of Stitching

For you to able to finish a line of stitching, pull the threaded needle across the back and weave the thread end through various stitches before clipping the thread.

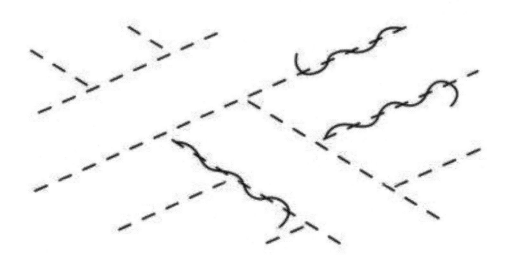

Tips

Ensure you always iron your completed work from the back to prevent the Sashiko stitching from crumbling or becoming too sparkling.

Sashiko Techniques

There are some fundamental strategies utilized in Sashiko weaving and it offers some helpful hints for making straightforward and upscale designs. Well, it might look muddled but, Sashiko is quite simple to learn and easily mastered. Since it is only an assortment of stitches of simple kinds, this strategy is fairly like sewing by hand.

There's a different kind of approach to stitching involved with Sashiko. Good practice is needed. In this case, the needle remains still and the fabric is worked onto the needle. Since you make a few stitches all at once, a long needle is exceptionally helpful. This is additionally why the fabric isn't placed into a hoop or edge. There is a particular reason a stitch isn't done at a time. This is because there's a tendency for the thread to twist. In this case, you take a stab at four to eight stitches for each inch so the more layers you have the more drawn out the length of the stitch will be. For moyozashi, there is a gap between the stitches and it is half the overall stitch length. It is significant when sewing not to cross the strings or make them have a form of contact.

Strategies for working

Transfer of Design

There are a few techniques for moving designs to fabric:

- For straightforward and recurrent designs, it should be drawn on the fabric, directly. This is done by the use of French chalk and a template, tailor's chalk or a water-erasable pen.

- A geometric design is then drawn directly on the side; the right, of the fabric, utilizing tailor's chalk and a ruler.

- Follow the plan on paper and pin to the side of the fabric, with the use of dressmaker's carbon paper placed between the paper and the fabric. The design is outlined with a dressmaker's wheel, a hera or a strongly pointed pencil.

- For fabrics which are thick and woolen, the design is traced on tissue paper and pin to the side. With tacking of small sizes, stitch round the design outline, utilizing a contrast color string; at that point cautiously tear away the tissue paper. After the work is finished, the small tacking should be removed.

Attaching the layers together

- The backing fabric; side, is placed on a level surface.

- The wadding (whenever needed) is placed on top and afterward the top fabric, right side up.

- Tack flat stitches of fastens to hold the three layers set up, working from the middle outwards. At that point tack vertical lines of sewing.

You can make Sashiko designs on patchwork and with appliqué, or as weaving on a solitary layer of fabric.

Quilting can be done through two layers. These two layers are top fabric and the backing. The wadding can be included, making three layers altogether. In other case, the completed bit of work can likewise be fixed with a layer of lining fabric. To expand or diminish the size of a design, move it to bigger or more modest graph paper, square by square, or your own graph paper can be made.

Setting up the Sashiko Thread

The skein is first opened and the band removed.

Search for the additional loop around the skein and slice through all strings.

Cut the opposite loop end.

There are two different thread bundles. One of the bundles is flipped at a degree of 180. There's a twist attached to the threads and this will guarantee the twist is going a similar route all through the bundle. Clutch the whole group and pull out one string, cut it into three pieces, and tie the pack in three places firmly with a square bunch.

There is a great tendency for the thread to fray, so use lengths of string no longer than 20-24" long.

Tips

The string pulls all the more easily and tangles less in the event that it is strung, so you are pulling with the twist rather than against it as you go on stitching.

On testing the twist, hold up a solitary string and squeeze near the highest point of the thread between your thumb and forefinger and move your fingers down the thread's length. In some way, it will feel smooth and at some times, it feels rough. A hued thread is tied at the highest point of the string bundle. Continuously pull your strings and from this end, thread your needle.

Step by step instructions to begin

A knot is created at the end of the thread and with this, stitch with the knot covered up in the fabric at the bottom. On the other hand, have the thread secured by making a couple of little fastens from the beginning stage and afterward sewing back once more.

Joining threads

The new thread is brought up from the rear of the work a couple of stitches before the end of the past line of sewing. Join along the current fastens to make the thread is well secured.

Wrapping up

Toward the finishing of the stitching line, sew back some small stitches in order to have the thread secured.

Sewing a Sashiko Design

You can have a thread pulled out from the customary Sashiko bundle or cut a 20"- 24" length of thread. This is threaded through the huge eye of a sharp needle, and makes a solitary knot toward the end.

Bring the strung needle up from the rear of the checked fabric on the background. Stitching can start at any point on the design; however, plan a sewing course that doesn't need an excessive number of turns, twists, or several skipped spaces seen at the back.

The point of the needle is placed level on the line of design at a short separation from where the thread arises, and measure. This causes you check how long the lines ought to be before you get it through the fabric. Holding the needle at an angle or in a straight manner before sewing a stitch can cause the point not to remain on line or you may misinterpret the length of stitch.

Tips

This Japanese technique of sewing involves keeping the needle still and the fabric is placed on it in a pleating manner. Put some light pressure on the texture and rock it, assembling a few lines onto the needle. On a normal note, the top stitch is somewhat more than the space in the middle. Be that as it may, equality is a higher priority than stitch length.

Have the needle pulled and to the knot, thread through. To the needle, take 2 to 3 stitches. The stitch length should be maintained at, 5-7 inches for each inch.

Subsequent to sewing an inch or two, pull up on the string somewhat; at that point, utilizing your thumb, cautiously loosen up the sewing. The thought is to keep the work free, particularly the thread on the back, so the sewing doesn't pucker.

Tension

It is imperative to keep an even strain all through your work. The fabric might get puckered if the stitching is quite tight. When it is loose and free, the sewing doesn't look proficient. A curve on the design or a long line of stitch? Create little circle of string under the bottom fabric or in between, if the kind of work done is the reversible kind. With this, the stitches won't shrink and pucker when washing.

At the point when you need to move starting with one piece of the design then onto the next, slide the needle under the backing fabric and at spans, create little stitches. For reversible works, slide the needle between the top and bottom material so the string will be undetectable.

Tips:

Customary Sashiko guidelines give point by point bearings with respect to the sewing courses to take and the quantity of fastens per leg of the design, yet as you gain insight and certainty, you will build up your own techniques. The principle concern is to keep the fastens even and the lines smooth.

Here are a couple of tips:

- At a corner, that's where a stitch must end, either with the string going to the back or coming up to the top. In order to sew curves which are tight, the stitches should be shortened.

- Strings that skip across the back ought not gauge longer than a large portion of an inch. Leave the strand free on the back to abstain from puckering. In some cases, a more drawn out skip can be avoided by weaving the string through a few stitches on the back to arrive at another segment of the design already marked.

- On ending a line of stitch, get the strung needle through the back and weave the string tail through a few lines of stitches prior to cutting the string.

- Continuously iron your completed work from the back so the Sashiko sewing isn't squashed or gets gleaming.

Setting up your Sashiko machine

You're obviously familiar with the techniques or weaving methods surrounding Sashiko; a form of embroidery done by hand and also having its origination from Japan. Observing the running stitches produces using the manual method, you'll notice absolutely no difference in that produced from the machine. This astonishing machine can do a wide range of things with this one basic stitch. However, one major challenge is the pricing. They can be somewhat expensive to purchase. Notwithstanding, you are bound to get some wonderful outcomes by using this machine.

Sashiko is restricted to one line of stitch; however, you can have a change of stitch by making use of the levers located at the front of the machine. You can decide to change variations on the stitch size; lengthening or making it short or you can decide on how the stitches should be spaced.

With the machine, it will be maintain, in a consistent manner, the uniformity of stitches, making it simpler and quicker to achieve your task. There's just one stitch required and it strings uniquely in contrast to a normal sewing machine since it just uses the bobbin thread and no top thread. However, it doesn't just take threading in the bobbin like you would on an ordinary machine. It tends to be somewhat complex until you get its hang.

The indigo-dyed fabric is the norm for Sashiko embroidery, coupled with white cotton thread. Well, with time, people delve into using different colors of threads and fabric desired. This evolvement also accompanied the use of the machine. Decorative form of stitching isn't the limit when it comes to Sashiko machine.

What's in the Box?

You'll happen to find these, when you get yourself a Sashiko machine.

- Sashiko machine
- Power string
- Foot pedal
- 3 spool covers in fluctuating sizes
- Sewing guide
- Larcel of needles
- Bobbins
- Cleaning brush
- Hook wires (which are important for the needle instrument)
- Tweezers
- 2 screwdrivers
- Guide for instructions
- Quick start aide

Setting up the machine

In the quest for setting up your machine, first of, choose a thread of medium weight as the Sashiko machine doubles up on the stitches. So in the event that you have too weighty a string, there will be constant shredding of the thread and constant issues with consistency of stitch.

On setting up, pick the hand-look quilt stitch. This is an option seen on the menu for quilt stitches. The selected menu is set up in such a way that there is pull up on the bobbin thread by the forward and back stitch to produce stitches which look more like it was done by hand. Choosing this stitch will likewise consequently build the top strain.

Circle round the bobbin with the thread, white colored, and place into the machine.

Wind a bobbin with the white weaving string and supplement into the machine.

The needle to be used is the size 100 topstitch. The bigger eye of the topstitch needle will give support to the monofilament string to run all the more easily, and a large needle possessing a large shaft makes a greater opening in the fabric, increasing the ability for the bobbin string to pull up more without any problem.

Using a monofilament thread, the top thread is threaded. There is a kind of difference between a monofilament thread and the normal one for weaving. This will be easily noticed if you haven't worked with one before. There's a feel of springiness associated with it. So, you'll need to be all the more careful and sew gradually.

Before you start sewing on your undertaking, do some test sewing on a piece of scrap. This will allow you to figure out how the stitch feels and how you want to go about working with it.

Start sewing, making the chalk lines already created as guides. In the event that you are doing the orange strip design, all straight lines are first stitched.

For lines which are curved, attempt to fasten as much as you can in one consistent line to get an appealing look. During the process of stitching curves, there may be need to take a slight pause and rotate your fabric periodically. Connect with the Needle Stop Down capacity and make use of the Free Hand System to lift your presser foot for simple turning.

Continue to stitch until you've covered every one of your lines. You can make use of this procedure to set up a pack board, quilt square, or clothing detail.

Ways to use a Sashiko machine

Sewing

In the event that you love the vibe of hand knitting yet don't have the opportunity or tolerance to sew a whole quilt by hand, you can do it with the Sashiko machine, all things considered. This is likewise an incredible answer for anybody with joint pain on their hands. With this machine, you'll get the vibe of hand knitting, however at multiple times the speed!

Appliqué

Want to make raw edge appliqué? The Sashiko machine can come in handy, for crude edge appliqué. This is a straightforward and lovely approach to appliqué your pieces down with a basic running create a form of fusion between normal Sashiko look and that of your appliqué project.

Adding trims

Applying trims to materials or decorative items in the home is one great use of the machine. This actually gives it a kind of look done by hand stitching.

Pleats

With the Sashiko machine, you can undoubtedly include a pleat on a garment or home decorative items. After deciding the position of the pleat on the fabric, align the fabric and raise it up against the needle. Secure using few stitches, then, proceed to press and join as you sew straight down. There you have it. A beautiful pleat made.

Learning Sashiko stitches

Sewing

- Weave stitches in such a way that they are even. Choose a particular length and work with it. Any lopsidedness will appear easily on the pattern.

- The quantity of stitches woven is seen to be more on the front side than the under. The overall proportion is 3:2.

- A length of 20 inches of the working thread should be maintained. This will make weaving easy and comfortable.

Step by step instructions to start, proceed, and end

- Bringing a line of stitch to a close, using a knot, is not allowed in Sashiko, normally. In any case, for its simplicity, we can make use of knots where the converse of the fabric won't appear. For fabrics where opposite will be appeared, utilize the conventional strategy as following:

- Make sure you stitch from left to the right side.

- Securing the thread comes with overlapping of few stitches. Make the effort of hitching the thread end at the other or reverse side.

- Trim the thread in such a way that it is close to the fabric to give a flawless appearance.

Making turns

- At the point when the designs are reversible, you need to ensure the back is neat. Thus, you need to remove the thread at every step of the way and shroud it under others. To accomplish this, follow a similar strategy as you would to start or end a stitch.

- With the fabrics reverse side hidden; you can turn utilizing a similar thread. You can convey the working thread at the rear of the fabric if the distance isn't in excess of an inch. Prevent puckering by making the thread loose. This is in respect to the carrying thread.

Corners and Centers:

- The corners ought to be kept sharp. To achieve this, weave in such a way that the stitch comes on the corner, that is, push the needle up or through the corner point.

- Leave the centers open.

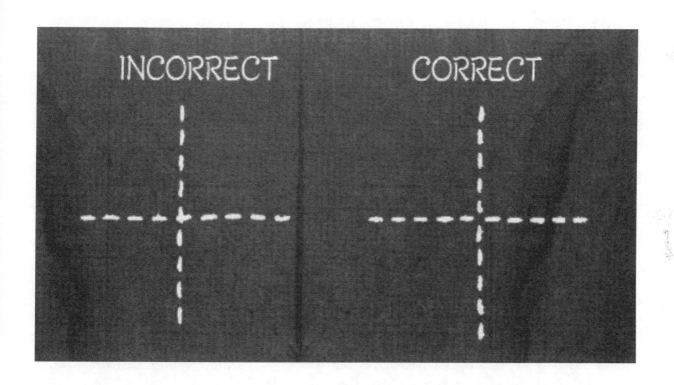

Appliqué and finishing

Regardless of whether you're have lots of experience or one who loves to experiment, the craft of applique is surely certain to come up in your practice. Appliqué is a form of decorative embroidery where different parts or patches in various shapes or pattern are stitched onto a bigger part to create an image or design. It is generally utilized as embellishment, particularly on articles of clothing. The strategy is pulled off by hand weaving or by the use of machine. Translated from appliquer, a French word, simply to mean, "To put on," appliqué is now and again used to adorn dress or materials. Like interwoven, it is a strategy for building or adorning quilts.

To enhance your applique, you can make use of distinctive colored threads applied around motifs, on its edges, and can even be decorated with beads or pearls. In addition to the fact that applique is a dazzling method to raise the aesthetic value of attire, it can likewise be applied to enhance bags, cushions and wares found in homes. The surface being fabric will go a long way in using applique be it with needlework or adhesive application.

With a kind of incline towards patchwork designs, appliqué designs were frequently propelled by regular daily existence, particularly the garden blooming with flowers. They likewise celebrated political and philosophical perspectives. Appliques created in the nineteenth-century were regularly made in bigger scope; as not many as four squares were required for a quilt of full-size. The twentieth century, particularly the Depression time of the 1930s, created its own yield of appliqué, regularly adorned with weaving and delivered in the pastels well known during the time frame.

How Appliqué Works

This technique is a moderately basic cycle with a wide scope of uses. One material is being appended to another. In this way, appliqué is started off with a base, the principle material being created. This might be a cover, a shirt, a potholder, or essentially some other human-made clothing material.

Apart from only attaching fabrics or materials to the other, elements for decoration can be included in the design. This technique is obviously for decoration, not simply a question of fixing openings or tear in your pants, so it's consistently critical to consider how joining things will affect the general outlook. Appliqué allows the craftsman to play with shading as well as patterns and fabric textures, making outwardly powerful materials.

Techniques for Application

There are three principal techniques for application with regards to kinds of applique, with every one of these having the option to make novel and various styles. The most widely recognized approach to join materials is with sewing, indeed numerous individuals characterize applique by embroidery. Picking a strategy for application truly relies upon the last look you're after and how exceptional your sewing abilities are, yet there's no set-in stone approach.

- Machine Applique

There are two primary techniques for finishing off applique by making use of your sewing machine. The customary technique (frequently called track down and trim) which is further developed includes sewing a position line, then place your fabric, bigger than the line over the stitches and afterward, to attach the fabric, a second line of stitches is created to hold the fabric in place with the material at the base.

A new and progressively mainstream strategy for machine applique is carried out with shapes already pre-cut, which can be laser cut or shop purchased. For the most part, a crisscross stitch is applied round the design edge. The edge smooth for the stitches to be applied and also, the shape is well maintained.

- Hand Applique

Most various assortments of applique are made with the aid of a machine. To create designs dimensional in nature and also quilt, you can make use of hand appliqué.

- Fused Applique

Applique weaving done the conventional way can be very tedious. To avoid this, many are tilting towards the use of fusible web. The web is a form of adhesive; iron-on. In case you're after a speedy method to make a compelling design, this technique is your smartest option. The web fuses the shapes to the base fabric and afterward, applies stitches with the machine to secure the fabrics together sewing.

Types of Appliques

Range of various kinds of applique exist; there's no correct method to explore the different avenues regarding this strategy, however, various techniques can bring about totally different looks. Pick the best style to upgrade your sewing project.

- Topstitch Appliqué

In this sort, the backing accommodates the appliqué; where it is stitched to. The too fabric gives the design layout while that of the bottom serve the field. This can be refined with two unique procedures using either hand sewing or a sewing machine.

- Cut Away

Different layers of fabric needed to make the design are briefly appended to a solitary layer of fabric which will be the foundation. After a successful transfer of pattern to fabric, sew it to join the layers. Cut of excess fabric to uncover the design.

- Pre-Cut Patterns

At first, decide on what or how you want the design to be. Cut the fabric into such and join with the backing. After attaching, sew the pattern to the backing of the fabric for your desired style.

- Reverse Appliqué

You'll require two layers of fabric; the top layer and the background layer. Place the layers on the main fabric. Texture is layered with a foundation layer of texture and a top layer of texture. The plan is sewed into the layers of texture and the overabundance texture on the top layer is removed to uncover the plan. In Reverse Appliqué either the top layer of texture or base could make the field.

- Needle-Turn Appliqué

This appliqué applies the procedure of cutting out already drawn pattern but in this case, some bits of materials are included outside the pattern already drawn. Sew the fabric, the pre-cut, to the fabric which is below, following the pattern lines and in the process of sewing down, fabrics in excess are turned below. With this, it is placed between the top fabric and base layers.

Finishing Styles

These styles of finishing can be used on the different appliqué kinds discussed above. You can make these styles with hand sewing. Some, however, will require the use of a machine to get a high level of precision.

- Raw Edge

Here, the raw edge of the fabric is seen to be revealed as an open stitch is used. The edge helps in pattern creation. An enormous assortment of stiches can achieve this.

- Finished Edge

A very tight stitch is used to enclose the edges of the fabric. The zig-zag or a satin stitch is applied.

- Whip stitch

This is fairly like raw edge applique. You're not too stressed over the edges and fraying of the edges can occur. You can keep the edge firmly secured to the fabric with a fusible placed under. This technique is majorly done by hand. You can use a machine but, you won't get the length and width mix that can easily be achieved by using hands to weave.

- Decorative Edge

The design is something in which the stitch is an intricate part of. One is actually allowed to see it. Generally the string is in a differentiating tone to the fabric and may even be an optional stitch. This form of stitch is usually decorative and there are huge varieties that can be utilized.

- Button Hole

This should be possible either with the use of hand or machine. There are a couple of sewing machines in which this stitch won't be offered, so, it is important you have that in mind when buying a sewing machine.

- Satin Stitch

There is a thin line between satin stitch and that of the regular zig-zag stitch. This depends on the proximity of the stitches when weaving. With your sewing machine, you can have good control over this stitch.

Sashiko Projects

Sashiko projects: one which requires few materials, can be seen anywhere and with this, the sanity of many have been saved. It is possible to create Sashiko pieces which are large and beautiful but having to settle with projects showcasing Sashiko's origin of designing objects of decoration seems natural.

Noren Curtain

Noren is a Japanese drapery regularly used to partition territories, for example, the kitchen from the front room. You will likewise see noren at the passage of numerous Japanese cafés.

You will require:

- Fabric (thick, woven texture both to obstruct light and look appealing from the converse side)
- Curtain bar
- Buttons and ribbons

Method: Get the measurements for your doorway; width and height. Gap the width significantly and add on 9cm at the top, 4cm at the base and 1cm on the two side edges for allowance of seam. Cut two pieces.

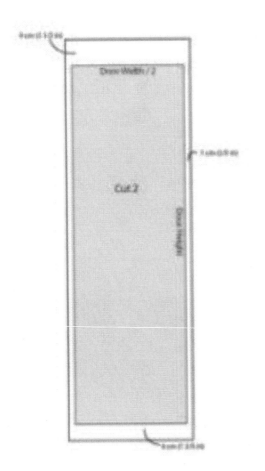 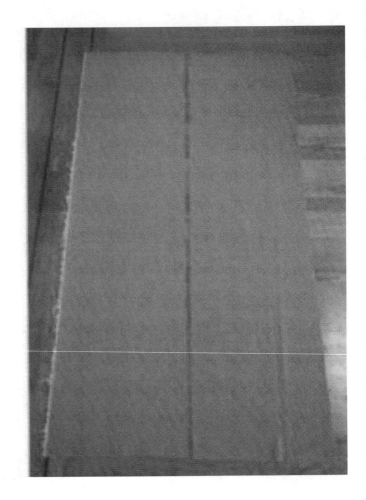

52

- At the right sides, fasten the top 19cm (9cm for curtain bar circle + 10cm for shut part of noren) to make the middle fold of the drapery. The 1cm seam is then pressed firmly, apart.

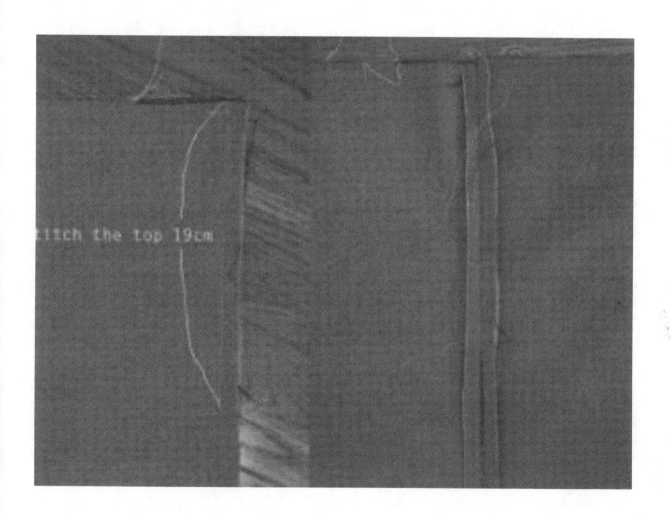

- Overlay and press the crease twice at 5mm spans to conceal the crude edge. A basting stitch can be done to hold the seam.

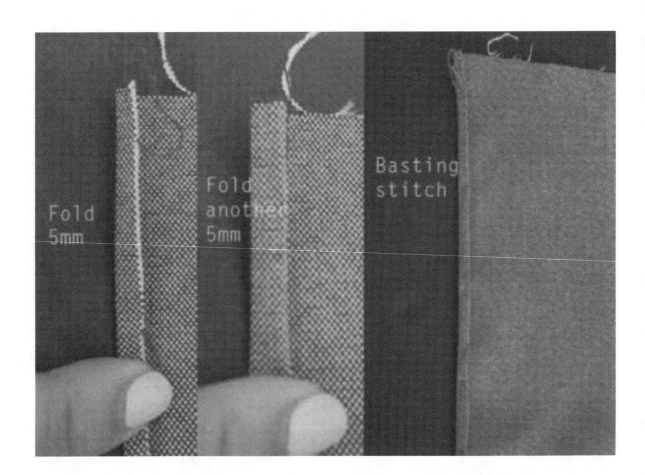

- Fasten seams and have the basting stitches removed.

- Do same for side edges. Crease and press top edge to 9cm imprint. Make sure the bar of the curtain fits perfectly, then, stitch.

- Trim the lower part of the curtain and you're done!

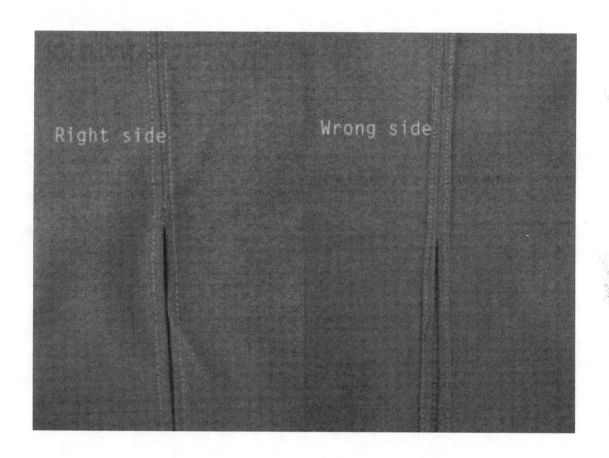

Right side   Wrong side

You can decorate your noren with beautiful buttons and weavings or leave it plain.

Sampler Cushion

You will require:

- Different arrays of coordinating fat quarters, fat eighths or large scraps.

- 1 meter of foundation and backing fabric.

- A 22-inch pad cushion.

In the event that you have marginally bigger or more modest pad cushion you can change the size of the sashing and lines to make it fit.

Method:

- Having looked up some amazing designs you can use for this project, make 9 of the designs measuring 6.5"block.

- Trim every one of your blocks to 6.5 inches square, at that point play with the design until you discover the one you like.

- The selvedges from the background fabric should be trimmed off and at that point, cut 4 strips from it, 1.5 inches' x width of the texture. These will be utilized for your sashing and boundaries.

For the strips, Sub cut them into;

- 6 x 6.5 inch strips (which are between blocks)

- 2 x 20.5 inch strips (sashing between segments)

- 4 x 22.5 inch strips (for borders)

- The columns should be joined by having the strips measuring 6.5 inches sown to the top and lower part of the middle block, at that point join the top and base square on the opposite side of the sashing strip.

- You can skip this step if there's no plan to quilt. If you'd prefer to stitch your pad front, cut a bit of wadding around an inch bigger than your pad front board on all sides. The edge of the cushion front is stitched round, inside the 1/4-inch seam remittance (so preferably around 1/8 of an inch from the edge). Cut back any excess wadding.

- Cut 2 pieces measuring 15 x 22.5 inches from the backing fabric, remaining.

By using your iron, press in one of the 22.5 inch edges by around 1/4 an inch. Crease it over and do it once more. This folding is repeated on the long edges on your other bit of fabric to have it secure, stitch the edge inside.

- The front panel of your cushion board is laid down, level, with the right side in the upward direction. The back piece is placed on top, that is, the side up. This is so the correct side is in contact with the right side of the cushion front. Line it up so the sides and base line up with the front board, and the stitched edge is in the center. By using your pins and clips, hold it in place.

The backing piece is laid same way but, in this case, lined up with the top and side edges of the front board. It should cover the base piece by a couple of inches. Pin or clasp into place.

Sew close to the edge utilizing a fourth of an inch allowance of the seam.

- With an over edge foot in your sewing machine, switch over to that and make use of it. Or then again you can utilize a tight crisscross stitch, or an over locker. Sew around the edge again to ensure it is secured.

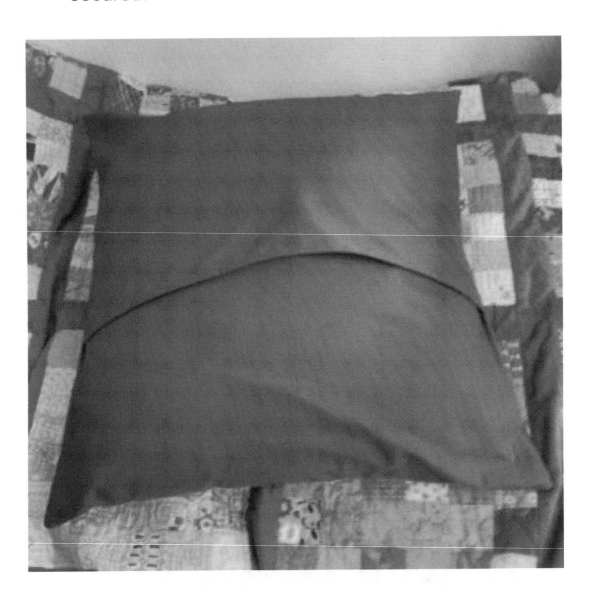

- Turn the pad cover through, jabbing out the corners. Stuff with your pad cushion utilizing the opening in the back.

Enjoy!

Sashiko Table Mats/Placemats

You will need:

- 2 1/2 yards of Kiyohara Linen Blend Solid in Brown, or other mid-weight woven cloth texture, similar to Purl Soho's Daily Linen

- Cotton Batting, Craft size, Mid space

- A 110-yard spool of Gutermann's Cotton Sewing Thread in shading 3630

- 4 bundles of Olympus' Sashiko Thread, 20 meters in Off White

- A hera marker

- Tailor's chalk

- A Sashiko needle

- A 25mm tape creator

- Safety pins, curve

Method:

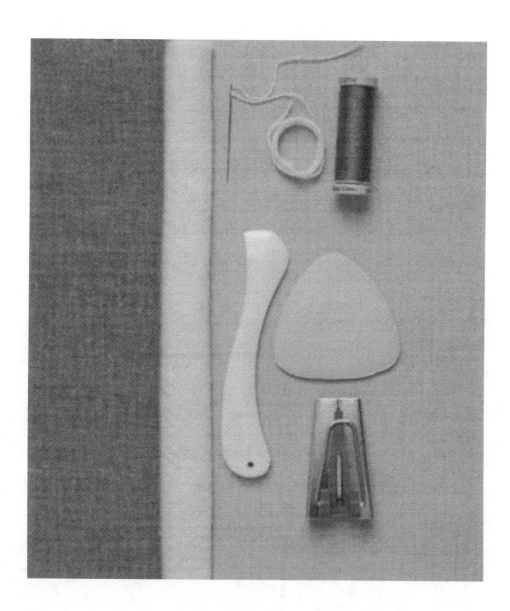

- Cut and imprint the pattern.

- The second material which is unmarked is placed on a level surface and ensures it's smooth and has no wrinkles. With the batting placed on top, smooth it down. At that point lay the top, stamped side up, on top of the initial two layers.

- Have the layers pinned together with few inches between. This is done with curved safety pins. Keeping the layers as level as conceivable as you pin.

- You will fasten along the vertical and flat lines taking stitches at every crossing point.

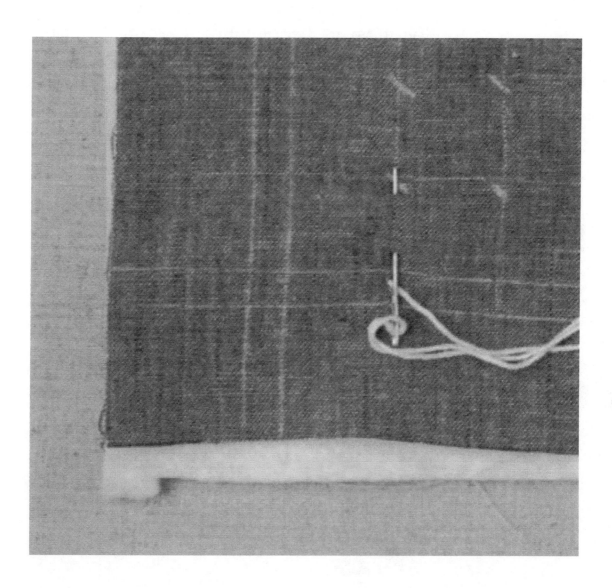

- Utilizing the Sashiko needle and thread, start the stitching at the posterior of blanket sandwich and exit not long before the sewing line at the lower part of the left most vertical imprint. Take a little running stitch, measuring around 3/8 inches in length at the sewing imprint, and afterward exit again not long before the following fasten mark. Take one more little running line at the stitch mark.

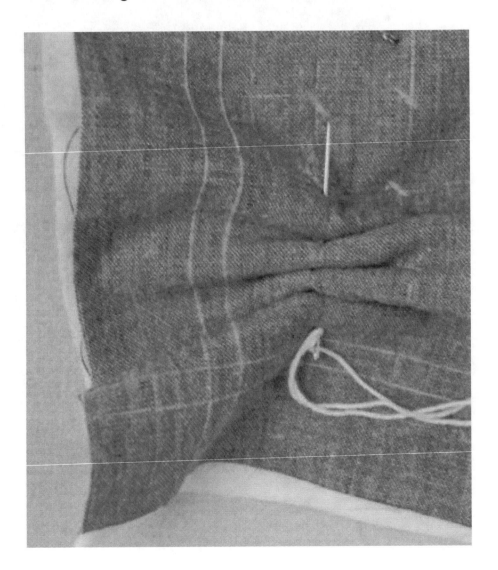

- Line along the whole stamped line taking little running fastens at each stitch mark

- Get the string through the lines and ensure the fabric doesn't pucker as this is done. On getting to the safety pins, remove them.

- At the point when you get to the furthest limit of each line of sewing, sew along the sewing boundary to the following checked line and start once more. Start and end the lengths of string simply inside the sewing line.

- Sew across the entirety of the vertical markings thusly.

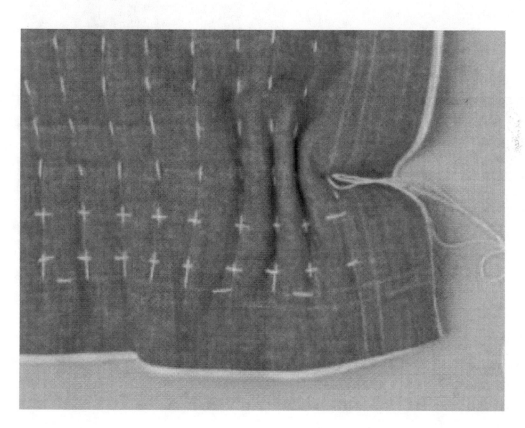

- Next, sew across the entirety of the even lines in similar way to make little crosses.

- At the point when you have sewed over each vertical and flat line, the front will resemble this.

What's more, the back will resemble this.

Sashiko Table Runner

This decorative linen is one several different ways to spruce up plain liners or tables which are bare.

You will require:

- Fabric

- Thread

- Scissors

- Sewing Machine

- Iron and pressing board

- Ruler or Measuring Tape

- Pins

Method:

- Measure out the width and length important for your completed table cloth, and add one inch to both.

- Cut the material to the required size.

- Iron your fabric. In the wake of pressing, a crisscross stich is made around the whole edge of the piece for a more expert look. The crisscross line likewise forestalls fraying.

- Go along the length of the texture, collapsing more than 1/2″ and pressing the crease level.

- The trickiest piece of this entire task is the point at which you arrive at the corners.

A 45-degree angle is first created by folding in the corners. Then each side is folded over with the goal that the different sides meet up in the corner at a mitered edge. You can make use of your finger or a pin to fold the excess material under the collapsed edge. A pin can also be used to hold the corners firmly until sewing is complete.

- Sew around every one of the four sides of the runner.

- Excess threads are trimmed off and you presently have completed decorative linen prepared for use.

Sashiko Purse

You will require

- Two pieces 4 1/4 by 6
- Two 2 by 6
- Two 2 1/2 by 6
- Two 2 1/2 by 6
- Fabric scrap
- Fusible fleece
- fabric, 2 pieces 6 by 6 3/4"
- One zip

Method: To start, your four pieces, which are obviously contrasting, are stitched together along the 6" edges; setting right sides together utilize 1/2" seam remittance.

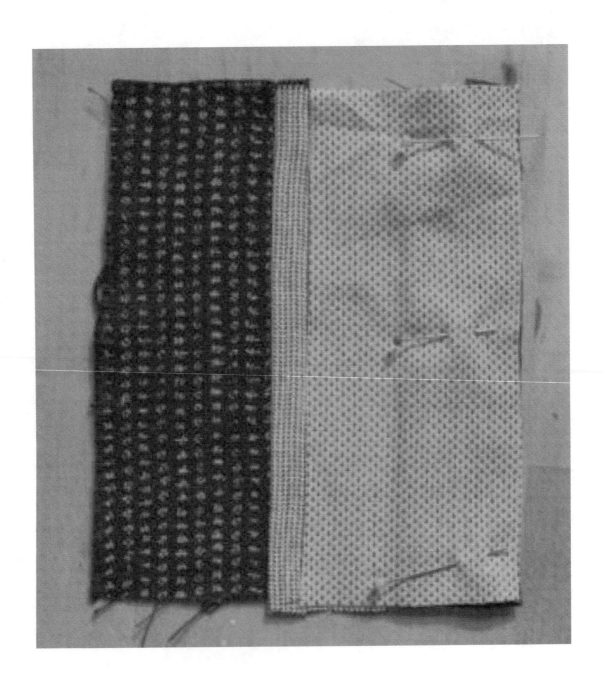

- For the second set of steps, repeat this process.

- Press.

- Working with the patchwork pieces, a fabric scrap is placed centrally on it.

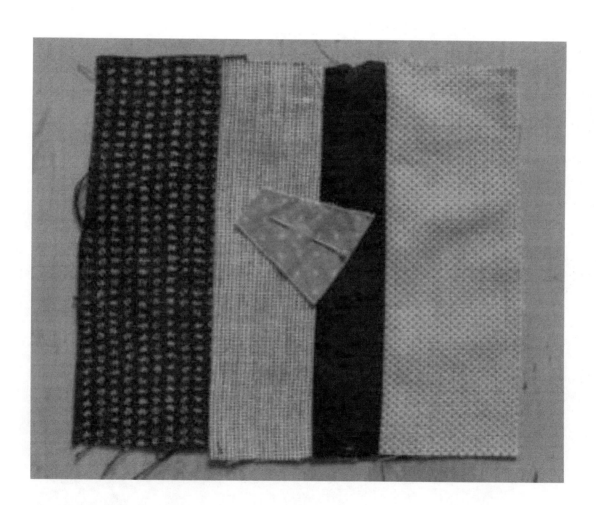

- Pin to hold set up.

- On using a running line start at the spot you wish to be the focal point of a hand-sewed circle.

- Utilizing a running stitch, sew from the middle to make a circle. Continuously work outwards until you have a satisfying circle in a differentiating line to your base fabrics.

- Pick one of your fabric pieces to add running stitch down the length of the piece.

- When your hand sewing is finished add fusible wool to the rear of your two interwoven pieces, adhering to the producer's guidelines.

- Close to manage your two out pieces and the two coating pieces to have bended edges.

- Trim your four bits of fabric.

- The right side of the lining fabric is placed up. The right sides of the zip, facing you, at that point the external bit of fabric side down essentially making a zip sandwich.

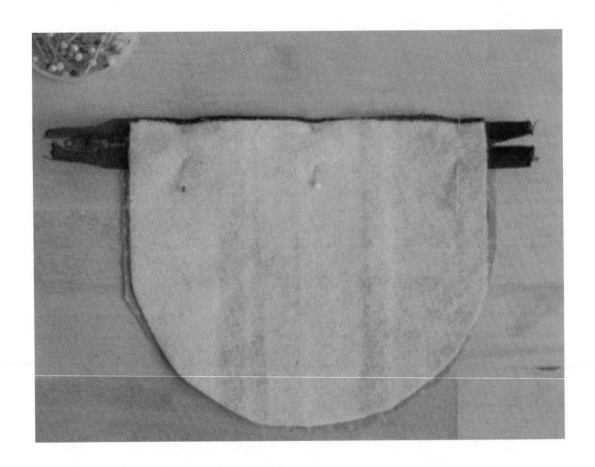

- Utilizing a zipper foot (in the event that you have one), line the zip set up along the straight top edge.

- Open out to uncover the zip and press. Pin the coating and top texture away from the stitch and top stitch.

- This is repeated for the second part of the zip.

- Open the zip midway (this progression is indispensable!).

- The fabric is then opened, so the two external bits of texture are on top of each, and similarly the two covering bits of fabric.

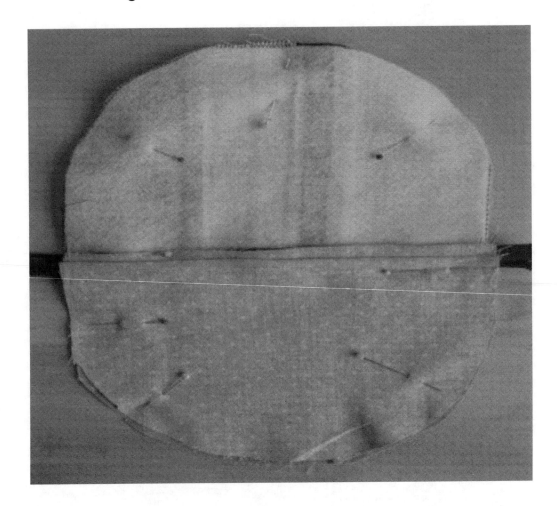

- Stitch in general, leaving a turning hole of 2″ along the coating.

- Turn right sides out.

- The gap in the lining fabric is ladder stitched. Push the coating back inside the charming coin tote.

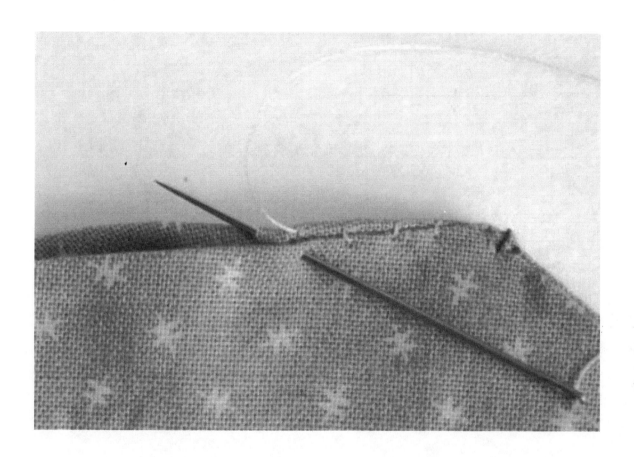

Sashiko Book Covers

You will need:

- Blue book fabric

- Velin Arches paper

- Acrylic ink

Method:

- Sheets measuring 4" x 6" (102 - 152 mm) are used for the book fabric covered book. Cut your book material to around 1" - 1/2" (25-38 mm) more extensive and taller than your sheets. Turn the book material over and draw around the sheets.

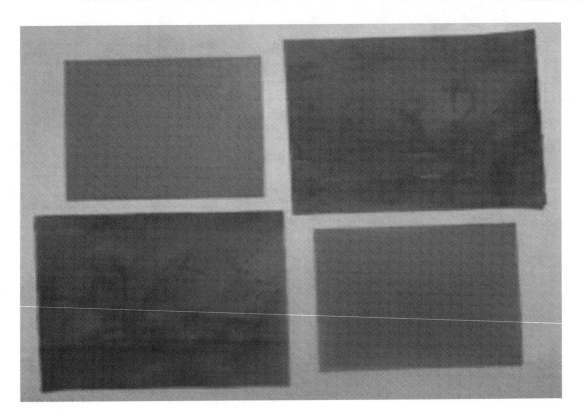

- Customarily, you would stamp out your design with a grid and uniformly measured stitches before you sew.

- A bookbinding needle, long in length, should be used and begin your sewing with waxed material string from the side.

- Wrap the sheets, including the end papers. Cut the endpapers 1/4" (6 mm) more modest than your sheets so you will have a 1/8" (3 mm) edge, Glue will in general leak through the sewing openings, so you can get waxed paper under the book fabric . This is done to have your work surface secured before you apply the paste to the back. Dispose of the waxed paper. Press the sheets into place.

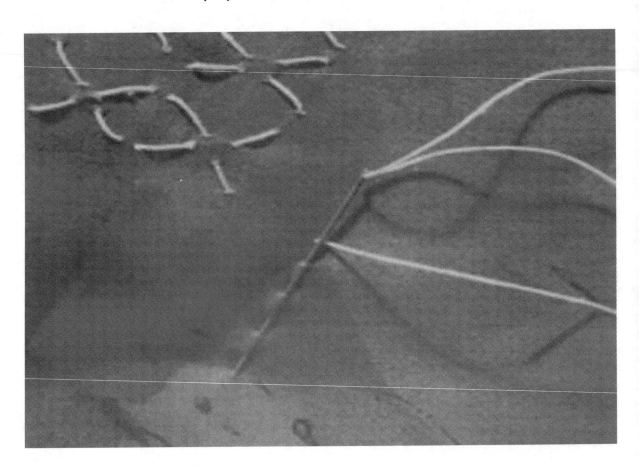

Sashiko Bottle Sleeve

You will need:

- Fabric scraps
- Scissors
- Sashiko needle
- Fabric marker
- Water bottle
- Ruler
- Cotton knit string

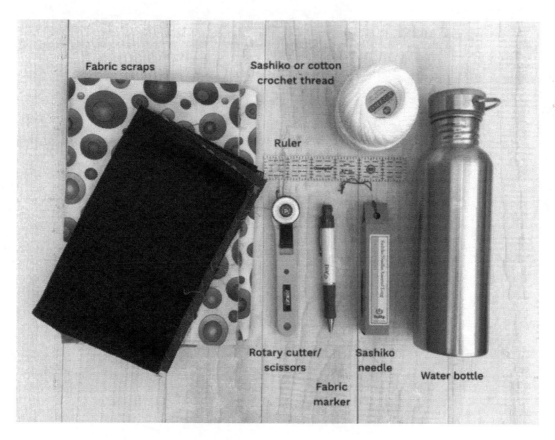

Fabric scraps

Sashiko or cotton crochet thread

Ruler

Rotary cutter/ scissors

Fabric marker

Sashiko needle

Water bottle

- Make a point to quantify the bottle's diameter. A form of seam allowance should be added to your estimation.

- With your favored fabric marker, follow the design on the denim. Make a 1-inch matrix. Draw an askew line on each square

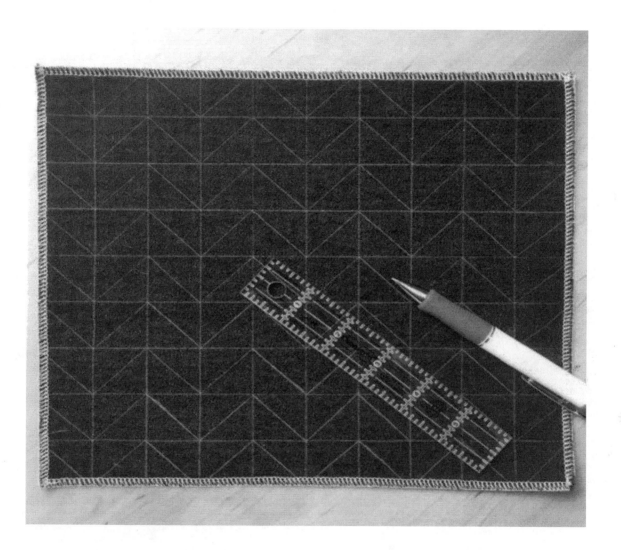

- With running stitches, sew horizontal lines first.

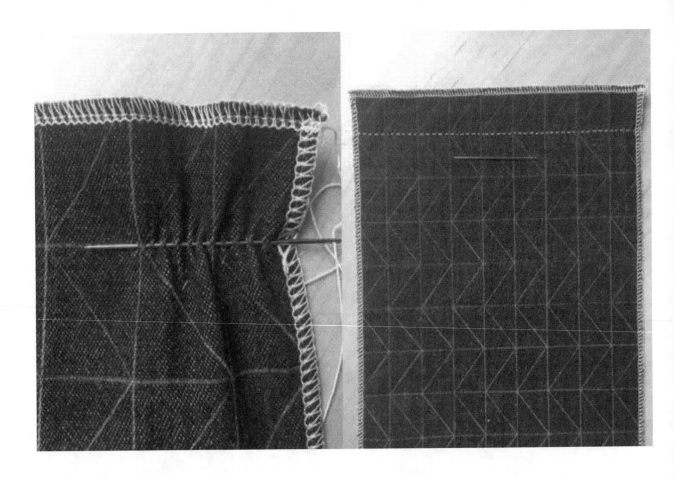

- Continue this process with the diagonal lines.

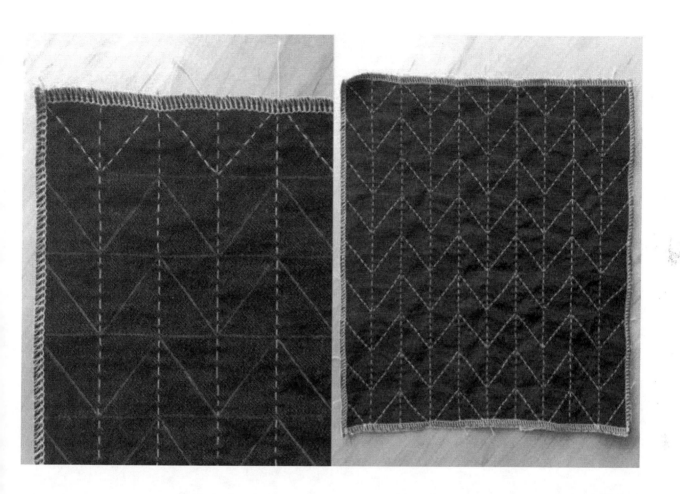

- There should be a fold of the right sides of the denim and sew along the edge. Spot the lower part of the cover inside the cylinder you just made and pin or clasp together. Do this for the covering also.

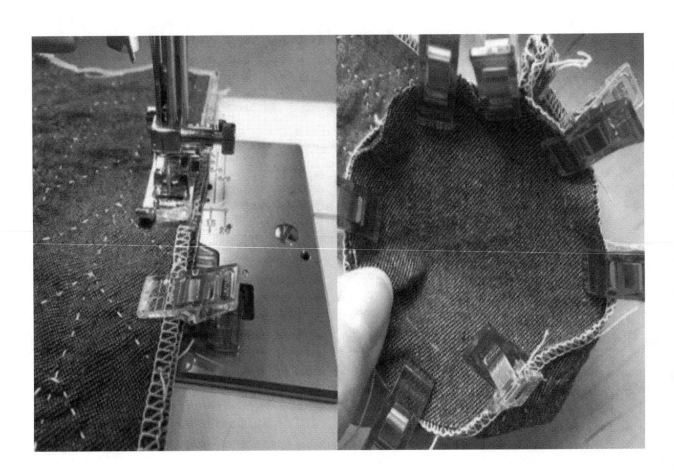

- Turn your coating piece right side out. Have it deposited inside the denim piece. Make a point to adjust the creases. Imprint a 2″ opening at the top. Sew along the edge.

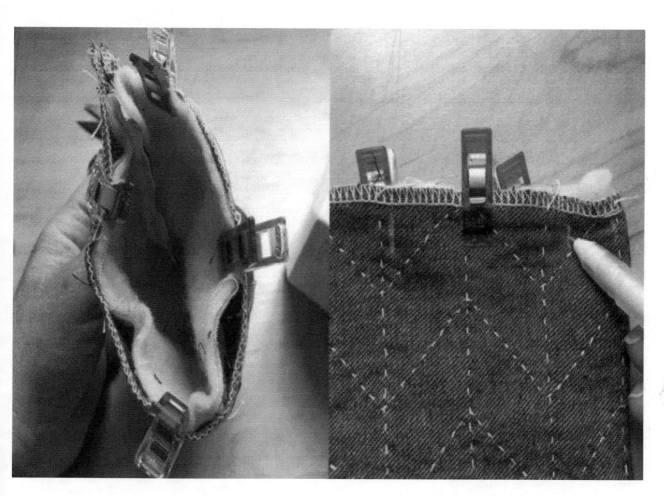

- Turn the cover back to front through the opening. Push the coating back in. Iron. Topstitch along the boundary is discretionary.

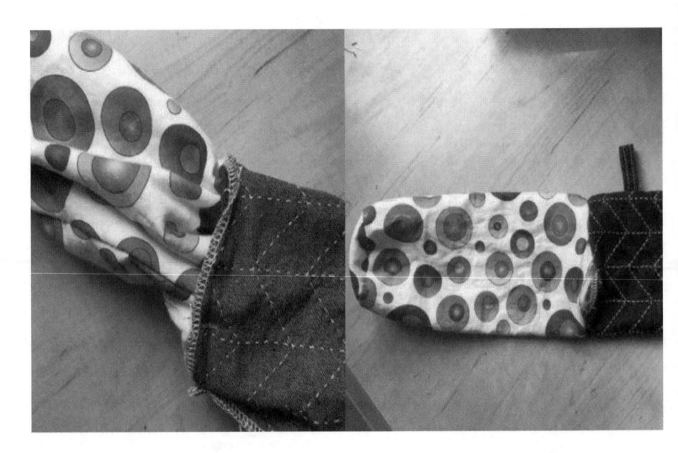

- Close the opening with ladder stitch.

Sashiko Napkin

You will require:

- Napkins
- Yarn
- Needle
-

Method:

- String up your needle with a long bit of yarn. Thicker fleeces look extraordinary however; you'll require a needle with a huge eye in the event that you need to use them. Beginning at one corner make a line and get the yarn right through until you have a couple of inches left on the tail. Keep on making a running line along the length of the napkin.

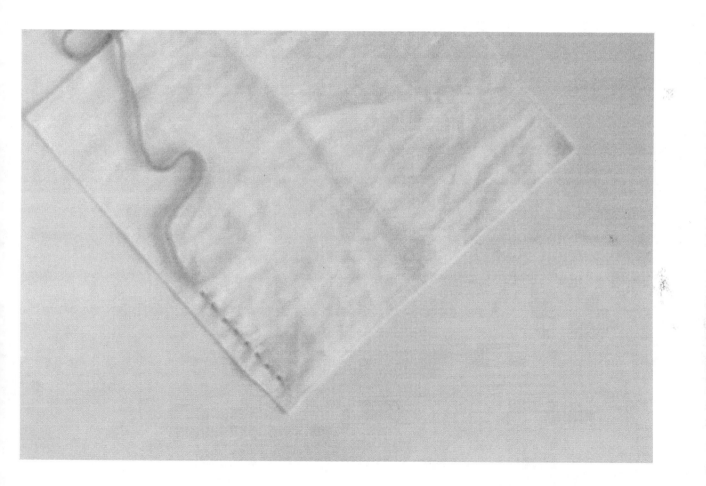

- Continue to go back and forth in rows format. Keep the sewing lopsided to make the Sashiko impact. At the point when you've sewn three lines, tie off the two ends and trim off the yarn in excess.

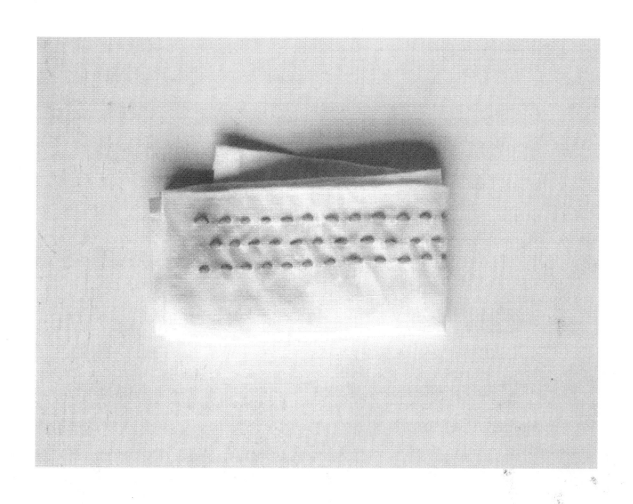

Sashiko Denim Tote Bag

You will need:

- Assortment of denim
- Weaving floss thread
- Cotton scraps
- Cotton texture for coating 5/8 yard or a large portion of a meter
- Two pieces of Annies Soft and Stable 16 by 18"
- Leather for leather ties, each estimating 31" by a 1"
- Leather opening punch
- Twofold cap bolts
- Two pieces of Iron on Interfacing 16 by 18"
- Scissors

Method:

- Make sure your interwoven design is somewhat greater than 16 1/2″ by 18 1/4″ (42 by 46 cm). Hold set up with pins.

- Handstitch the design, making use of running stitch.

- This should be repeated for the second side. Be certain, you can alter your perspective on string shading decision or bearing of sewing.

- Whenever you have finished your different sides, make use of glue spray to join the Annies Soft and Stable to the side of each piece. Have the denim pieces trimmed to the edges of Annies Soft and Stable.

- The two sides, which are the right sides, are placed together. Line around the sides and the base. Guarantee your crease is 5/8" (1.5cm) to be sure about Annies Soft and Stable is set up.

- Box the corners. In order to perform this task, force the base seam to meet the side seam and pin to hold.

- Utilizing a knitting ruler mark a join line at right points to your base.

Assembling the Sashiko Denim Tote Bag

- Pit the covering inside the denim external sack so the right sides are together. Pin to hold firmly and afterward stitch along the top.

- Turn through. Slip stitch the opening in the base crease of the covering.

- Top stitch the highest point of the pack, this will have the lining and the bag well secured and fortify its opening.

Adding Straps to the Bag

- The leather straps are cut out, estimating 31 by 1" (79 cm by 2.5cm).

- These are placed on the bag and held firmly with clover cuts. Poke two holes for each tie with an opening punch and secure the lashes set up with cap bolts.

Sashiko Mug Rug

You will need:

- Fabric scraps.

- Use cotton, cloth, or denim.

- Sashiko or sew string,

- Sashiko needle

- Fabric marker

- Ruler

- Thread

Method: Have the Persimmon Flower stitched. Cut a 6×6-inch bit of fabric. Follow a 1/4-inch matrix.

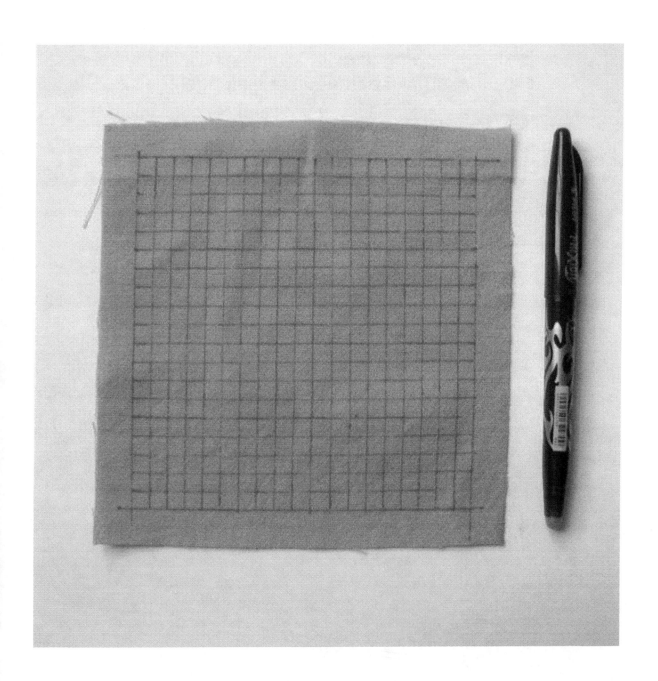

113

- Start by sewing the flat lines. You'll line two in a similar example, at that point a staggered line.

- Keep sewing the vertical lines.

- Your completed piece should resemble this.

Sashiko Sampler Potholders

You will require:

- Low space cotton batting
- Cloth or cotton texture
- Safety pins
- Sashiko string, or weaving floss
- Sashiko needle, or long needle
- Fabric marker or chalk pencil
- Scissors
- Ruler
- Straight pins
- Cotton sewing string
- Iron and board
- Optional: tear-away stabilizer, indelible marker, thimble, sewing machine

Method:

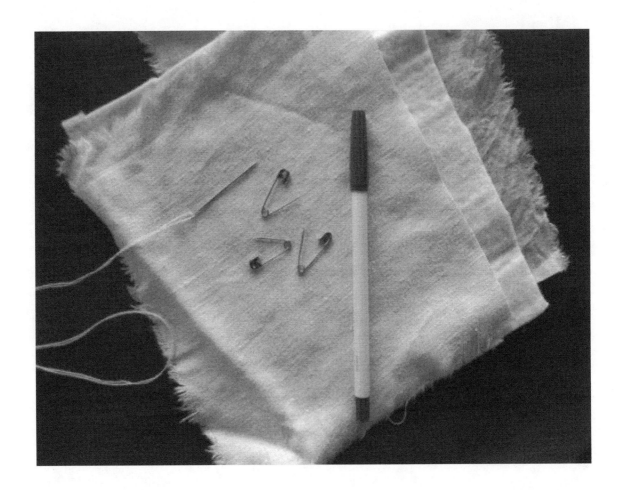

- Have your fabric pre-washed. Cut two bits of fabric and one bit of batting to around 8" square. Place the batting in between the fabric then use safety pins to hold the layers in place. The pattern should be drawn out or fasten the stabilizer.

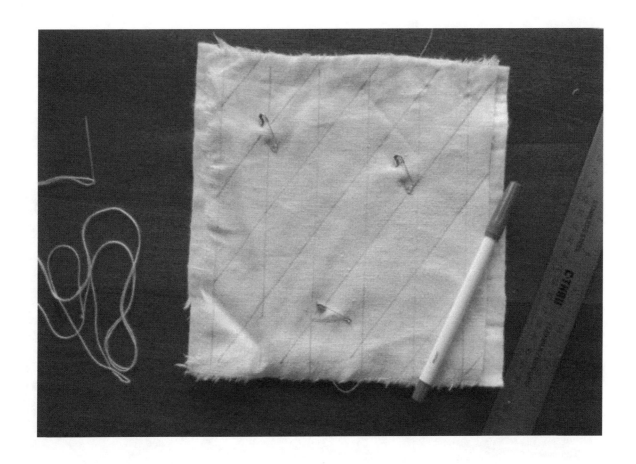

- Shroud your knot between the fabric and batting. With the pattern directive, sew a running stitch which should be large and (pretty much) even stitches through each of the three layers of fabric and batting.

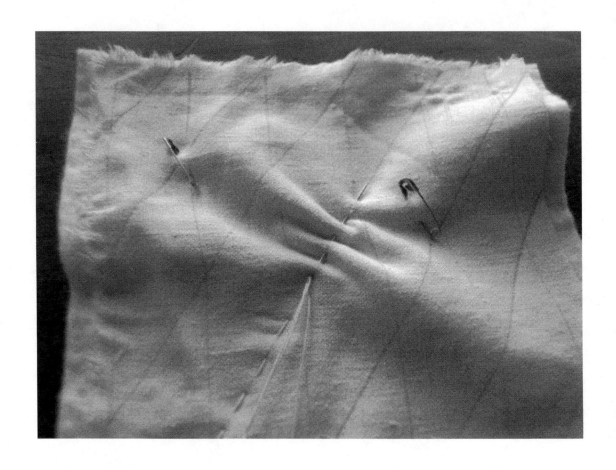

- When the Sashiko weaving is finished, tie the edges of the potholder. Cut a couple of long segments of fabrics around 1 3/4" wide. Combine two strips if important to stretch around the edge of the potholder

- Sew the coupling strip around the edge of the potholder 1/4" from the edge. If preferred, you can make use of a sewing machine.

- For adding fabric loop: Cut a bit of fabric 1" wide by 3" long. Crease the long sides to the middle and press, again, fold in half and press. Sew down the length of this and make it into a circle.

- Cut around the edge of the potholder (and end of loop) flush with the edge of the coupling strip, 1/8" from the crease. Rearrange the coupling strip so it folds over the edge of the potholder to the front.

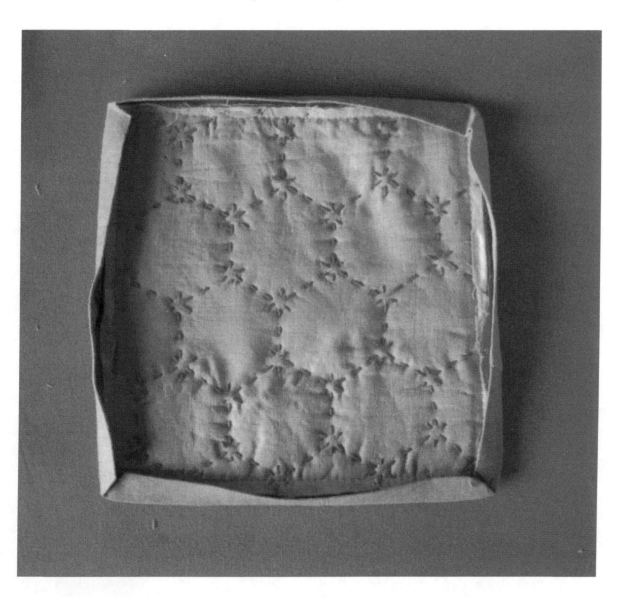

Sashiko Cushions

The pillow size is 20"× 20"

Materials Needed:

Panel embroidery:

- Natural fabric(22")

- Sashiko thread and needle

Pillow completion:

- Fabric for back of cushion is 22

- Zipper(17.5")

Steps:

1. Draw a square at the center of the fabric. Make sure the square is 2 inch smaller than the finished pillow size. Drawn 20 by 20 squares for the project.

2. Draw vertical guidelines at 1/2, 1/4 and then 1/12 of the width.

3. Horizontal guidelines should be drawn at 1/2 and then 1/6 of the vertical length.

4. Draw the Sashiko pattern. Yellow chalk can be used on the black linen fabric to make it really stand out.

5. After drawing the pattern, start stitching. You can start with the outer square border, followed by the vertical and horizontal lines, all in white thread. The diagonal lines should be stitched using two different shades of blue thread. The stitches should be kept slightly longer than the gaps between the stitches at an ideal ratio of 3:2. This means that the gap between the stitches should be 1/3 of the length of the stitches themselves.

6. The pillow should be stitched together and the zipper attached as you would with any standard pillow. And that's it! Your beautiful pillow is ready.

Sashiko Coaster

There is no such thing as a perfect size for a coaster, so you can cut the fabric as you like.

Materials Needed:

- Front fabric and the back fabric
- Interfacing
- Sashiko thread
- Sashiko needle
- Thimble
- Scissors

Steps:

1. Choose a pattern, transfer the pattern to the front fabric and then stitch the design on the fabric.

2. After stitching the front fabric, place the interfacing on it.

3. Iron the interfacing on the front fabric.

133

Place the back fabric on the front fabric (the side on which the interfacing is ironed).

4. Use pins to hold the back fabric on the front fabric.

5. The pins should be placed on the corners of the fabric to hold it in place.

6. Stitch around the corners of the fabric and turn it.

7. Since stitching around it is the finishing part, you can make a knot.

8. Trim the sharp corners after stitching around it.

9. Flip it to reveal the side of the front fabric without the interfacing.

10. After stitching, use the needle to bring out the corners properly.

11. A sewing machine could also be used to stitch around the corners.

12. Stitch the side that you used in turning it to close it. This should be done neatly.

13. Your Sashiko coaster is ready for use!!

135

Sashiko Sunglasses

Materials for sunglasses case

- 22cm×12cm pieces of base fabric.

- Patches of Fabrics of preferably rectangular size for Boro work.

- Contrasting colors of Sashiko Thread or Perle Cotton for Boro stitching

- 2 pieces of lining fabric 20cm by 12cm

- Two pieces with two scraps of iron on light weight interface so that it strengthen foundation fabric 22cm by 12cm

- Magnetic Clasp

Steps:

A seam allowance of 1/4 inch should be used all through.

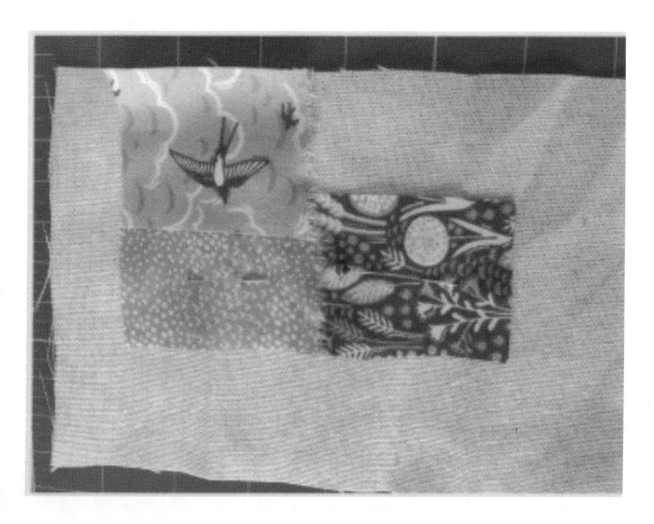

Making the Foundation Fabric

Adding fabrics for Boro work

Press the piece of calico and then start by adding small rectangular pieces of fabric. Pin in place and make the raw edges to show to give the work an aged look. Add more patches and tile then over the previous pieces. Secure the pieces in place with running stitches.

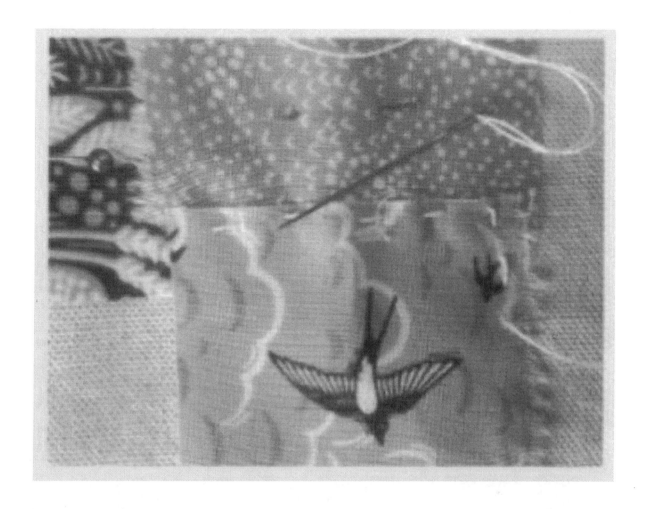

Boro Stitching

Knot your thread and hide the knot behind a fabric patch. Take stitches down edges of fabric patches. The size of the stitch depends on your preference.

Finished Boro stitching

Ensure that the base pieces of calico are completely covered by adding more pieces and stitching them. This will form the foundation fabrics for the outer part of the sunglasses case.

Interface is then ironed to the right side of each piece of foundation fabric to strengthen the fabric

Lining and main fabric aligned

To secure the ends, take piece of fabric and place right sides together with Boro fabric piece along short edge and then stitch along. The same should be done for other pieces and the seams pressed towards lining fabric.

Attach a magnetic clasp

Add the magnetic clasp to the lining pieces. The central point should be Measured at least 2cm from the top of the lining fabric and then a scrap piece of interfacing fused to the fabric. Two small slit should be made using a ripper tool. Then one half of the magnetic clasp should be pushed through holes while ensuring the clasp is right way round on interior of lining fabric. This should be repeated for the other half and making sure they properly aligned when closed.

Making a sunglasses case

Press the two stitched pieces and arrange them together with outer pieces facing each other and the lining pieces facing too. Use pins to hold them together and then stitch. 5or 6cm gap should be left in the lower edge of the lining fabric for turning through. Securing stitches should be added at the different ends with the seam allowance kept towards lining when sewing.

The corners should then be snipped and care taken not to cut the stitching.

Slip stitching

The case should be pushed through to the right side. Make sure you slip stitch gap in lining with hand to produce neat finish..

Inside of sunglasses case

Finally, push the lining inside the case. The more you use any Boro fabric, the more it frays thereby giving it a nice look.

Denim Repair (Boro)

Materials Needed:

- Sashiko thread
- Sashiko needles
- knuckle ring thimble
- Pieces of fabric
- fabric pins
- fabric marker or chalk
- ruler (optional)
- scissors

Select your fabrics and then cut into desirable shapes that are at least an inch larger than the opening in the denim. The fabrics should then be inserted into the leg of the jeans.

The fabric should be aligned under the opening with at least an inch extra on all sides. When patching denim around knees, give center of fabric slacks in order to prevent tear.

Pin the fabric into place. Stitch in any direction or pattern. The needle should be inserted through the denim without pulling the thread. Continue running the needle through the denim, while holding the denim and fabric together.

The thread should be pulled out when you have many Stitches on the needle.

This should be continued until the end of the row and the other row should be started, going in the opposite direction.

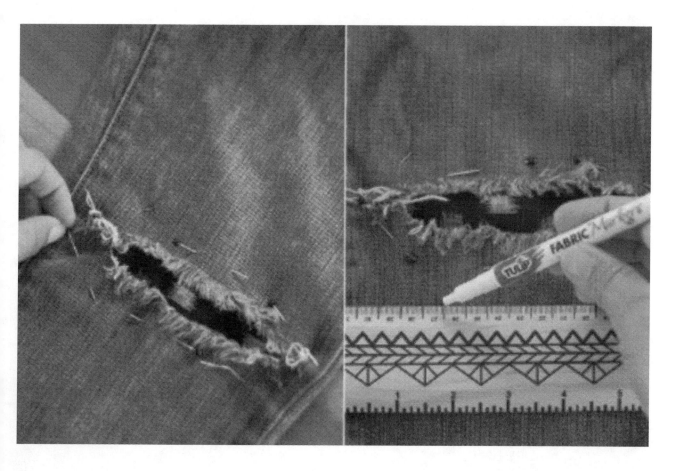

Tie off thread when you get to bottom of ripped opening then begin again at top, as you work downwards. You can stitch around or over the fabric.

Patches can be stitched over the rips too. Play around with the positions and stitching!

This will give you a perfect denim mending.

Heart Needle Book

- Materials Needed:
- Download the templates
- Cotton or light linen
- Scraps for details
- Matching and contrasting thread
- Button
- Embroidery thread
- Batting or felt
- Light weight cardboard
- Ribbon
- Gluestick
- Patch and appliques: needle book pages

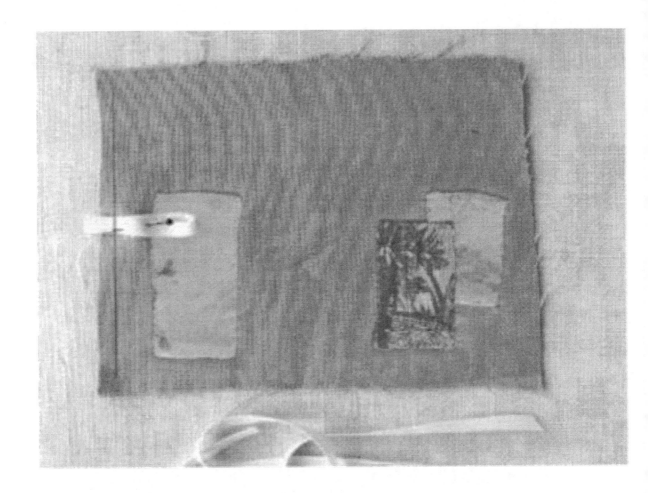

Cut out pieces A, B and C plus the heart pieces. Use one side of Pieces A as the cover page.

Put patches, I embroidery, and others to the pages.

Two support pieces should also be cut out from lightweight cardboard.

With the help of a glue stick, the cardboard should be glued to pieces of batting and then cut out.

Cut out a length of ribbon measuring 3 and 1/2 inch and then fold in half. The folded ribbon is then affixed to the center of the left side with pins

Ensure that the folded edge extends 1 and 1/4 inches from the seam line. You can use 1/4 inch cotton twill tape.

Attach all the pieces together (A, B, C and heart pieces) right sides together using pins. Then all the seam lines stitched together with small section left for turning. The opening on A should be made large enough to insert the cardboard supports

All the corners of the rectangles close to the seam should be clipped off. This same thing should be done to the bottom point of the heart and notches around the around the curves at the top and center.

The main step is to turn al the sewn and clipped pieces right side out. A chopstick can be used to push the corners and curves all the way out. At this point you can now add any additional appliqué or details.

Batting pieces and cardboard should be put into cover page such that batting side faces in side and cardboard faces outside cover.

Cardboard can be pushed all way to each side then empty space should be left between them, then ensure cover is open at bottom.

Stack the pages with the ribbon loop on the right and then fold the book in half.

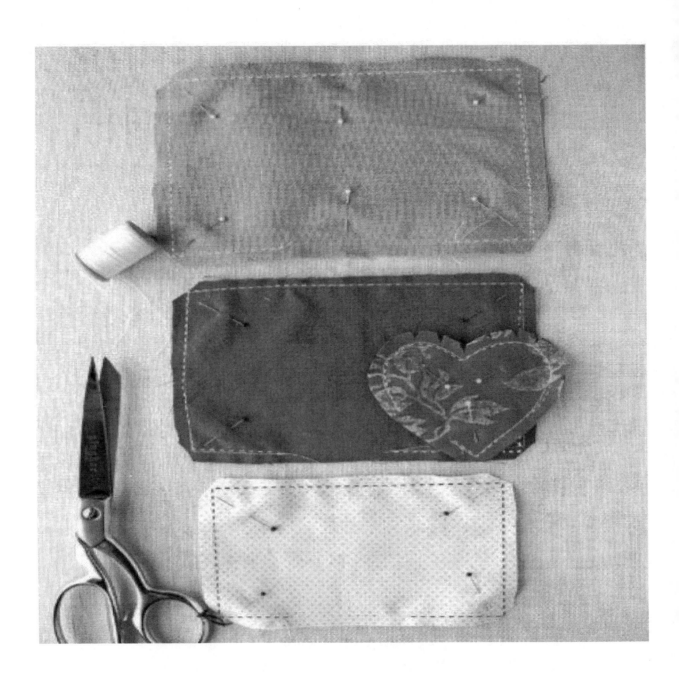

Determine the position to put your button by folding the loop up over the cover. The buttons should then be stitched in place. Appliqué can be used to cover the knots, if you stitch through the cardboard.

Each of the pages should be stitched close and then pressed. Move on to finish the page edge.

Use blanket stitch on the edges of each page with embroidery thread. One of the stitches should be made perpendicular to the edge with a knot at the top. The needle should be inserted away from the edge and about 3/8 inch from the first stitch. The needle should be brought through the loop and the thread pulled tight.

In assembling the book stacks, the loop should be on the right hand side. The pages should also be put in the center and held in place with several pins

The bottom of page B should be attached to the inside of page A at the center with few stitches. The center top should be stitched as well. Stitch the center top as well.

Matching thread with the blanket stitch of page C should be used and page C attached to B at the top and bottom center.

The top and bottom center of the heart should be stitched to page C using matching threads with the heart edge stitches.

Stitching should be done all through the heart while catching the top layer of page C.

This will give a finished work. You can now add all your tiny projects, scraps and sewing tools when you want to travel.

Sashiko kid cloth mending

Materials Needed:

- Patch
- Item to repair
- Embroidery or small sharp scissors
- Fabric scissors
- Cotton embroidery floss or sewing needle
- Printable sticky fabric-solvi stabilizer
- Sashiko needle

Steps:

A 1/4"or 1/2"grid should be printed onto an adhesive stabilizer. The patch fabric and stabilizer should then be trimmed to fit the melding area.

The patch should be pinned in place and hand basting done around the entire area with the running stitch and sewing thread.

The stabilizer should be measured and cut out to fit the working area. The backing should then be removed and out on top of the patch and the item mended.

The pattern should be drawn on the grid to make it easier to sew. Ensure a washable marker is used.

The zig zag pattern is interesting and easy. It has a lot of Stitches to cover all the worn out areas of the denim with time as the jeans are washed and worn. When you are through with all the steps, simply wash the jeans and the stabilizer will disappear.

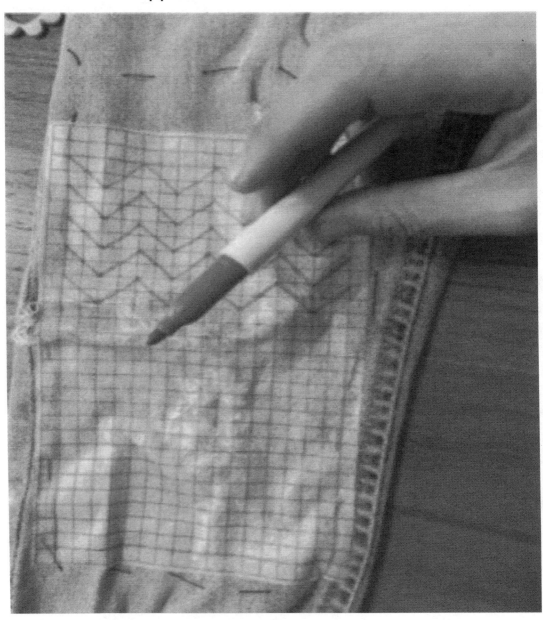

Brooch

A brooch is a piece of women's jewelry having a pin that allows it to be fixed to clothes mostly worn on the upper part of the body; also referred to as "Breastpin".

Materials Required:

- Metal bezel setting with pin back (different kinds of cotton fabrics)
- All kits such as Liberty of London and Echino or Japanese prints
- Natural Cotton Batting
- Sashiko Yarn and Needle
- Glue
- Original Sake Puppets Patterns
- Transfer Paper
- Scissors
- Thread

How to Make it:

Step 1: - Gather your Materials as you arrange them accordingly

Step 2: - Simply Stitch some Fabric Pieces Together

Step 3: - Add some Sasho Details

Step 4: - Assemble Settings by Using the Included Materials; remember that patterns and design ideas are included.

Step 5: - Make it to a size of 1 1/4" X 1 3/4" (that is 32 mm by 45 mm). The choice of selecting fabric may vary according to your preference.

Sashiko Denim Bag

Is fun working with denim, because it is so versed, mostly available - your friends and relatives can help you with their old pairs of jeans? But if donations from friends are not possible you can get fairly used ones at the shops near you.

Materials Required:

- Embroidery Floss Thread

- Cotton Scraps

- Different Kinds of Denim

- Cotton Fabric for Lining 4/7 yards

- Leather Hole Punch

- Double Cap Rivets

- Annies Soft and Stable, 2 pieces 16 1/2 by 18 1/4" (42 by 46cm)

- Leather for Leather Straps, each Measuring 31" by a 1"

- Iron on Interfacing, two Pieces 16 1/2 by 18 1/4" (42 by 46 cm)

How to Make it:

Step 1: Denim Tote Bag

Arrange some pieces of denim and cotton patched in a design so appealing to the eye.

Make sure your patchwork design is a little bigger than 16 1/2" x 18 1/4" (42 x 46 cm). Use pins to hold in place.

Step 2: Sashiko Stitching

Use a running stitch to hand stitch. What I have been using is a split embroidery floss thread with that I had fun with various colors. But on the alternative, you may prefer to use a traditional Sashiko thread.

It is always good to be creative while working, give a thought about the direction of your stitches. I mostly prefer my stitches to run horizontally. However, I always emphasize the cotton patches with vertical or circular stitching.

Do the same for the second side of the bag. It is left with you now to make use of the color varieties or stitching directions.

As soon as you are done with your two sides apply some craft glue spray to hold the Annies Soft and Stable to the left side of each piece.

Your denim pieces should be trimmed to the edges of Stable and Annie's Soft.

Place the two right sides together.

Stitch within the base and sides.

To secure Annie's Soft and Stable in place, maintain your seam at 5/8"(1.5cm).

Ensure the corners are boxed. To achieve this, raise the base seam to meet the side seam and hold the pin.

Mark a stitch line at a right angle to your base with the help of a quilting ruler.

The seam space is to be trimmed, this is the main body of the completed bag.

Step 3: Lining the Tote Bag

The heavyweight interfacing to the back of the lining fabric should be ironed.

Cut the fabric, as you prepare two slip pockets, 7 x 6"(17 x 16cm).

Turn over the top of the pocket twice and stitch.

Fold and press two times the sides and base.

166

Pin at the center on your lining approximating 3" (7.6cm) down from the top of the bag, then stitch.

From the top, centrally insert magnetic snap.

Stitch the side seams and across the base.

Ensure you create an allowance for turning out across the base seam.

Box the corners

Step 4: Assemble the Sashiko Denim Tote Bag

The lining inside the denim outer bag placed so the right sides are joined.

Pin into place and then stitch across the top.

Because of the bulk, I recommend a walking foot and a long stitch.

Turn all around. Slip stitches the opening in the base seam of the lining.

Stitch the bag from the top, this will put the main bag together and strengthen it at the opening.

Step 5: Adding Straps to the Bag

Cut some leather straps measuring 31 x 1"(79 x 2.5cm).

With clover clips, place the leather straps on the bag and hold in place.

Puncture two holes per strap with a hole punch and safeguard the straps in place with cap Rivets.

Flat-Sheet Duvet Cover

To make a customized summer-weight comforter cover from two new flat sheets is amazingly simple-and cost-effective. All you need do is to partner up different shades. For added ease, leave the normal button closures at the bottom and add grosgrain-ribbon ties. This easy, low-cost cover will aid in keeping your duvet neat and will remove the necessity for a top sheet as well, this implies that your bed will be easier to make.

Materials Required:

- Flat Sheets

- Pins

- Comforter

- Sewing Machine and Supplies

- Iron and Ironing Board

- Sewing Thread (matching color sheets)

- Fabric Scissors

How to Make it:

Step 1: - Choose 2 flat sheets that are a similar size as your comforter (for instance, for a twin-size duvet cover, use two twin-size flat sheets).

Step 2: - As much as possible, cut sheets so they are 2 inches wider each than a comforter and 3 inches longer (to give allowance to seams)

 Step 3: - Position sheets so that finished top edges match together and wrong sides facing in.

Pin and stitch (using a 1/4-inch seam space) within three edges, the edge of sheets having 1 inch, finished top edge is left unstitched which serves as the opening.

Step 4: - Turn the duvet cover inside out, then press a 1-inch seam with an iron, pin and sew, only overlapping the spacing of the first seam.

-Turn off the right side of the duvet cover; press again.

Step 5: - To Hedge duvet-cover opening, if you want, turn a 1-inch width under once, then again, making one complete fold.

Sew top and bottom together at each corner of the opening, about 20 inches towards the middle, allowing a gap that is large enough for a duvet to fit through.

Step 6: - Cut out 10-inch lengths of ribbon.

Pin one piece of ribbon to the top and bottom sheets, at approximate 5-inch increments, flap inside of the openings.

Sew on ribbons; remove pins.

Step 7: - Slip in Comforter and tie the ribbons.

Sashiko Patchwork Bag

This is an organic, inspirational Japanese patchwork and Boro technique. The reason why I cherished these methods is that it is environmentally friendly: in terms of reuse, recovery, and recycle phenomenon behind them, and I made use of some of my fabric scraps that have piled up the years in my house. I looked for little pieces of blue fabric to use.

Materials Required:

- Sewing Machine
- Sewing Threads and Needle
- Pins
- Some pieces of fabric
- Hot Iron
- Scissors
- Zippers
- Some Lengths of Brown Leather strap Material

How to Make it:

Step 1: - I started with ripping some of the bigger pieces up into little segments and making some worn patches.

Then is time to play around with the pieces, layering and overlapping them to make a large patchwork rectangle.

At this stage, I will be using pins to adhere it all together before I begin to stitch.

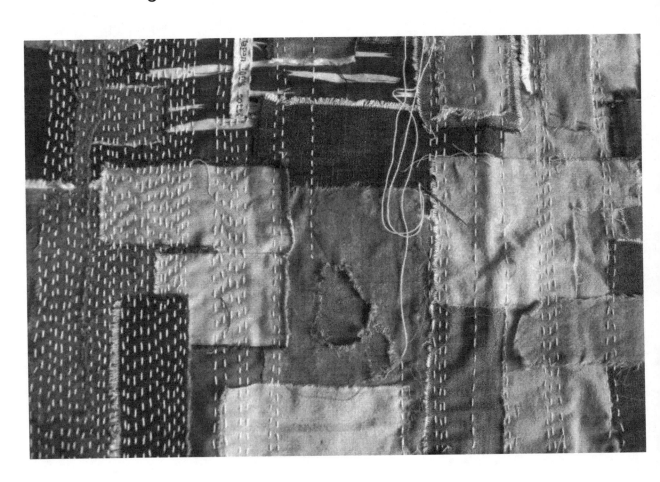

It will be wiser at this time to lay out the pieces on fusible interfacing and then iron, this will help to hold most of the pieces in position.

Step 2: - I would be running a stitch throughout all the layers to hold everything together and to reinforce the fabric.

Step 3: - With my skeins of thread that will run out about 2cm away from either edge, this seemed unimaginable, so this became the size of my completed bag.

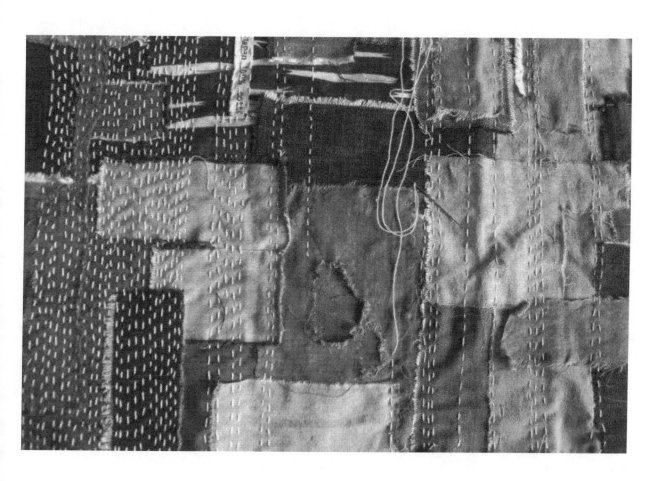

Step 4: - At this time I ironed on some lightweight interfacing and then folded the rectangle I got into half seaming down both sides and then start pinching the corners to make a boxed shape of a tote bag.

Then is time to add a recessed zipper

And again an internal zipper which forms a pocket for keys and wallet, made of yellow cotton.

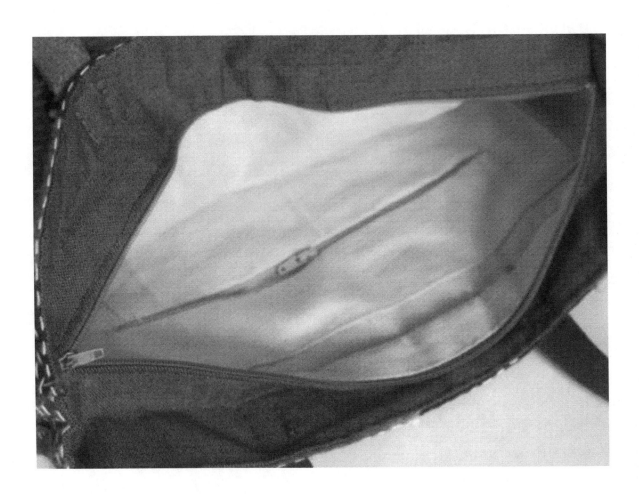

Step 5: - In maintaining the spirit of reuse, I have to make of use an old strap from a long worn-out bag to create the handle. As you can see in the picture below, there are buckle holes all over the handle, but never mind it still looks fine.

Japanese Bound Book

Stab Binding allows you to create books that are almost impossible with other types of bindings. For example, in a pamphlet-stitch book, every leaf, or page, doesn't have a separate color.

But as for the stab-bound book, you may apply scraps for various weights, colors, and textures provided they are of the same size or could be cut to the same size. If you want to start a scrapbook project, then this is the perfect idea for you.

Materials Required:

- One roll of unbleached French Linen Thread

- 10 Sheets of 7" by 9" Paper for Pages

- 2 Decorative Sheets of 7" by 9" Paper for Covers (you can purchase yours at Morita Washing in Kyoto, Japan; at an affordable price.

Other Required Items:

- One Steel Ruler

- One Pair of Scissors

- Gauge bookbinding 3 4/9" by 21 needle (Blunt tip is better)

- One Binder's Awl; mostly used for the piercing of Sewing Stations

How to Make it:

Out of the four basic variations of Japanese stab bind, I shall be focusing on the most common and popular one being "Yotsume Toji".

Step 1: - With a pencil and a ruler, mark 4 sewing stations. The 4 sewing stations should be at least 1/9" from the spine edge. (Mine is 1/3" from the spine edge). Station 1 is at least 1/3" up from the end; Station 4 is at least 1/3" from the beginning. Stations 2 and 3 are spaced equally between.

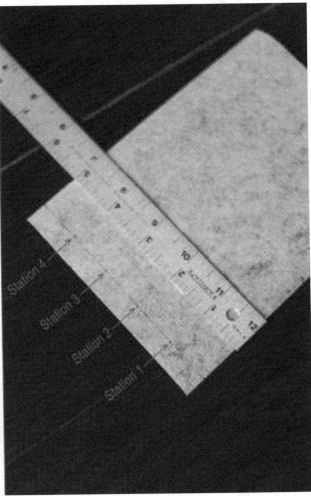

Step 2: - With your awl, pierce sewing stations. How to pierce through this book bulk is quite challenging.

Some bookmakers prefer a drill or a nail and hammer for this particular task. You are to mind your fingers. I used a low-cost binder clip to hold mine together.

Step 3: - Thread your needle and tie a knot at the tail end.

Step 4: - To bind, start from station 2 (back cover side).

Pull your needle across station 2.

Pull snug too.

Step 5: - Your needle should be wrapped within the spine and back through station 2.

Step 6: - Bypassing through station 1, wrap the needle within the spine and back through station 1.

Step 7: - Needle should be wrapped across the head to front cover. By going through station 1.

Step 8: - Pass through stations 2 and 3 simultaneously.

Step 9: - Pass through station 4.

Wrap across the spine and back through station 4.

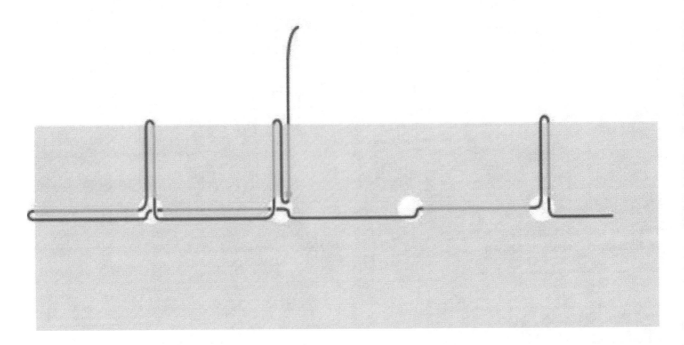

Step 10: - Wrap across the tail end to the front cover.

Pass through station 4.

Step 11: - Pass through station 3.

Wrap across the spine and back through station 3.

Step 12: - Pass through station 2.

Tie a knot in square form.

Sashiko Kinchaku Drawstring Bag

Kinchaku is traditional Japanese purses or handbags. It is a small bag, mostly combined with a drawstring. Others say Kinchaku are purse or lunch sized drawstring pouches. They were traditionally made with Chirimen. There is a variety of designs and materials for Kinchaku available.

Most often, they are made with fabrics, sometimes the same fabric as your kimono. This bag can carry a whole lot of things ranging from gym clothes, toothbrush, lunch, money, shoes, luck chains, and many more.

This project is really fast and uses up smallish bits of leftover fabric.

Materials Required for Embellishment of the Pouch:

- A Yo-yo
- A Button
- A Patch, it could be purchased or handmade from a piece of fabric.
- A little Embroidered thing
- A Ribbon Flower or Bow
- A Small Applique thing

Basic Measurements and Specifications:

For a basic pouch, you will require the following fabric -

- 1 cm (0.5 inch) seam allowance.

- Finished pouch, width - 12 cm, height - 16 cm, and depth - 5 cm (5 x 6.5 x 2 inches); this could be made of different sizes, just subtract or add the width, height, and depth to reflect your current reality of size.

- For the lining: 1 piece measuring 17 x 34 cm (7 x 13.5 inches)

- Drawstrings: 2 pieces, 2.5 x 20 cm (1 x 8 inches)

- Pouch exterior: use 1 piece measuring 17 x 45 cm (7 x 18 inches)

- While for the drawstring casings: 2 pieces, 3.5 x 15 cm (1.5 x 6 inches)

How to Make it:

Step 1: - Fold one of the drawstrings into half, lengthwise.

Press and open out and fold the edges towards the center, so that they could meet at the crease you just created by pressing in.

There should be another again within the first crease, encasing the edges.

Stitch down to the center of the drawstring. Repeat to create the second one.

Step 2: - Complete the casing of the edges.

Turn under 0.5 cm (1/4 inch) on all the edges and press.

Step 3: - Mount the casings.

Put one of the casings at the center of the pouch exterior, making a parallel to and 5.5 cm (2 and 1/4 inches) from one of the short edges of the pouch exterior.

Pin in position.

Stitch across both long-time edges and not across short edges, this is where the drawstring is expected to be inserted into the casing.

Repeat with the second casing across the other short edge of the pouch. In case you are using some form of embellishment, is time to add it, and the position should not be more than 5 cm (2 inches) from the base of one of the casings.

Step 4: - You will pin the lining to the exterior, as the right sides are facing each other - short and edge of lining to the short edge of the pouch.

Stitch, then repeat with the other short end and press seams open. You can see pouch/lining seams pressed open below.

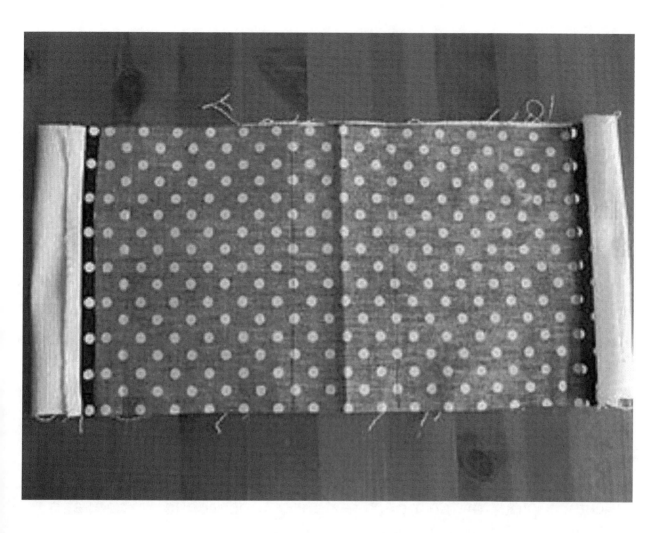

Step 5: - At bottom of the lining and bottom pouch, make pleats.

The pouch/lining should be placed on a flat surface and gently line up the seams you just pressed open, ensure they are together then pin.

Turn the end of the pouch closer to you and draw a line of 2.5 cm (1 inch) up from the folded bottom.

Flip to the other side of the pouch and do the same thing.

Turn the pouch within and repeat these markings at the end of the lining.

Open out the pouch and fold, right sides together across one of the markings.

Press. Fold and then press open along the other three lines you just drew.

Then line up the folded edges at the pouch end, right sides together, and then pin.

With a pleat of the pouch exterior sandwiched in between the folds. Repeat the same at the end of the lining. Check out the picture below for a "sandwiched" pleat of fabric.

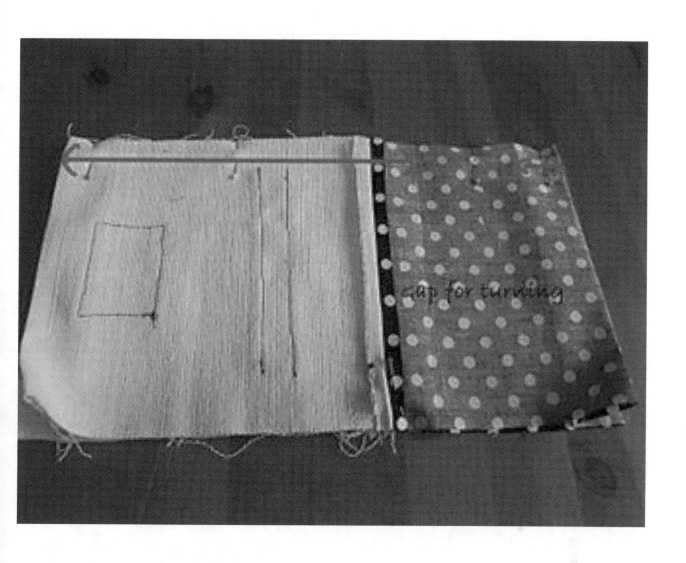

Step 6: - One long edge of the pouch) the lining should be sewn. Sew the other side as well, but leave a 5cm (2 inches) space in the seam, at the end of the lining, securely backstitch where you stop the stitching at each end of the space.

Through the space provided, turn the pouch/lining right side out.

Push the lining into the bag. Since the lining was not as long as the pouch, which is about 2.5 cm (1 inch) of the exterior will turn into the interior part of the bag.

At this moment, you will poke out the bottoms so that they look like this one in the picture.

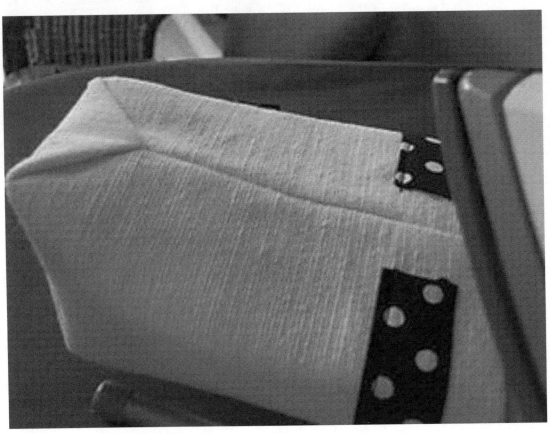

Step 7: - Input the drawstrings as shown in the photos below.

Then tie a little knot at each of the drawstrings ends, like what we have.

Pass one of the drawstrings across the casing on one side and continue across the casing on the other side. Look at the photos below that is how the drawstrings should be.

Before you will be sure you are through, you have to go back and sew that little space you kept earlier for turning.

Sashiko Knee Patch

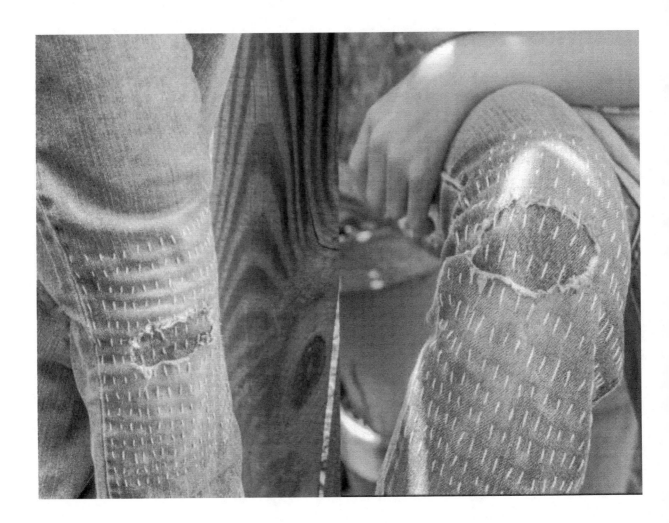

This style of noticeable mending was mostly used in Japan to repair kimonos. The embroidery serves two purposes: the primary purpose is to reinforce a worn out area of the clothing and secondly to add attractive design to it.

This technique is very simple and requires no special tools.

Materials Required:

- Long Embroidery Needle
- The Fabric for Patch
- Scissors for Cutting
- Cotton Embroidery Thread (optional embroidery floss)
- Fabric Soap or Chalk (for ruling)

How to Make it:

Step 1: - Clean the Torn Area and Cut the Patch

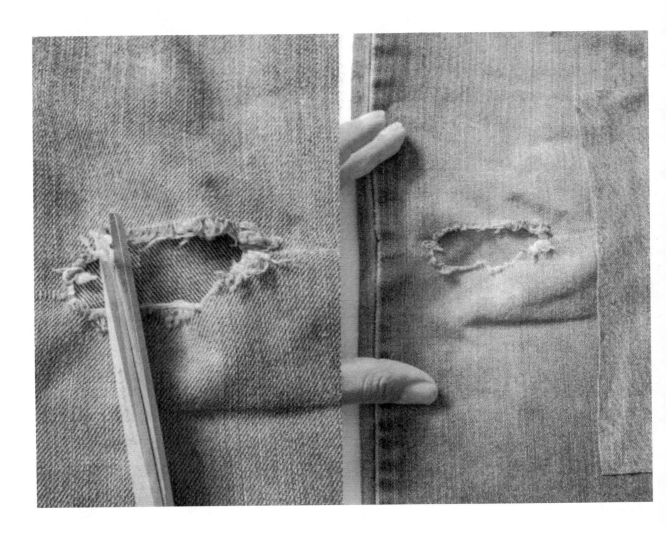

Remove the threads within the hole.

Use a fabric remnant to cover the holes beyond the torn area. But the fabric should be of the same material and color as the torn clothing.

As to ensure that the knee doesn't continue to wear out, make sure the piece of fabric covers the whole worn-out area and beyond.

Step 2: - Apply the Patch

Apply the patch inside the pant leg, ensuring the whole area is properly covered.

Pin the patch in position. While you are pinning, do not pierce through to the back of the pant leg, only the upper layer and patch underneath.

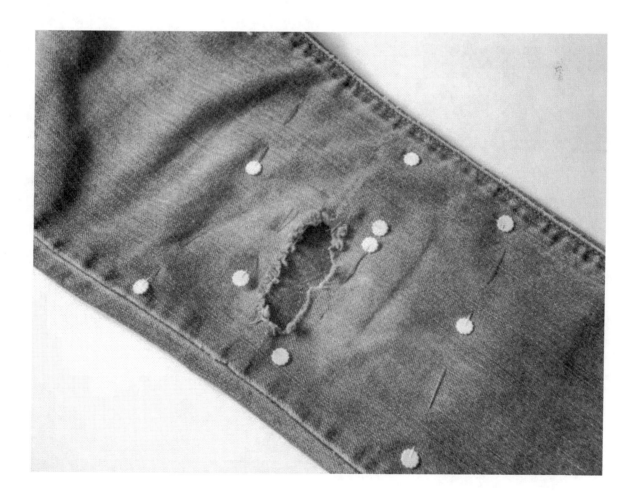

Step 3: - Mark Lines to Sew

The easiest, to begin with, it is a straight line. To ensure your lines are straight, measure, and mark parallel lines within the knee area on the pant leg.

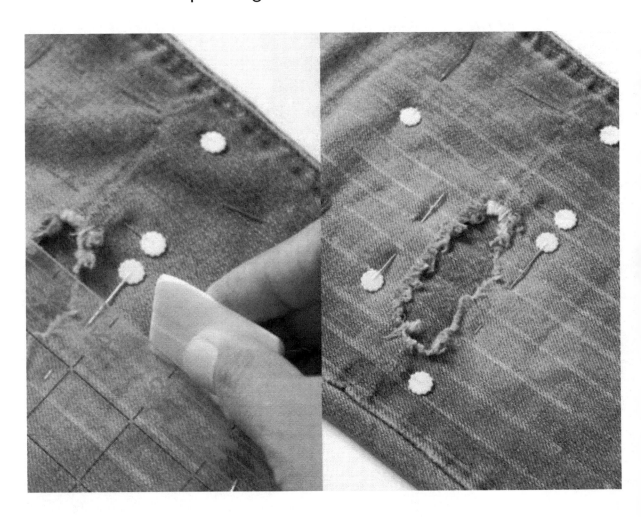

Step 4: - The Sewing Begins

Cut about 20-24 inches of thread. Ensure you maintain the length at that if not the thread will tangle as you progress in the sewing.

Tie a knot to one of the ends and apply the needle through the base of one of your lines which are closest to the edge of the pant leg.

Run the thread across the patch fabric and the top of the pant leg.

With a "running stitch", apply the needle across the fabric without pulling the thread through. Maintain the stitch at about 1/4-inch long.

Run the needle across the fabric until you have various stitches on the needle. If even they are not uniform no problem but for neatness and attractiveness, you can maintain a good straight stitch.

Immediately you approach the end of the line, ensure you end each row with the needle on the underside of the patch.

Begin the next row by bringing the needle up crossing the top of the next line.

Step 5: - The Finishing

In case you are out of thread while sewing, knot the thread underneath the patch.

It will very easier if you change the thread at the end of the row.

As you continue sewing, stop every stitch and smoothen the fabric out to remove the folds and squeezes from the fabric.

Scrap Fabric Bracelets

If you have been collecting fabric, then you will realize that it's pretty difficult to throw away any leftover pieces of fabric from your sewing project.

Every little fabric scrap matters a lot is saved with the hope that it could be useful again sometime.

These scrap fabric bracelets are one of those projects you could use them for. You can go through your scrap bag; it is to time to put them to great use.

Materials Required:

- Sewing Machine and Accessories
- Lobster Clasps
- Iron
- Scrap
- Sew-in Interfacing
- Ribbon Crimps
- Pliers
- Jump Rings

How to Make it:

Step 1: - Take Measurement

With ribbon crimps, determine how wide you could make your fabrics. Give an allowance of 1/4-inch seam on every side.

Length of fabric. Use a strip of fabric to measure the size of your wrist and next add a 1/2 inch.

You should cut the interface to the same width as the ribbon crimps.

Step 2: - Begin the Cutting

Cut two people of fabric and interfacing for each bracelet. You may choose to use different fabrics for the back and forth to make your bracelets reversible.

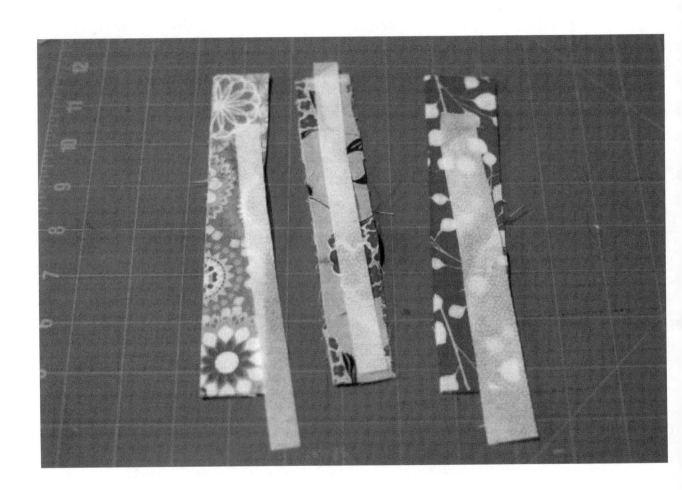

Step 3: - The Sewing Begins

Sew down through the center by placing the strips of interfacing at the center of the wrong side of the fabric.

Sew the remaining side as you have done

Iron the 1/4-inch seam space kept for both sides of the bracelets.

Bring the right sides of your fabric strips together, ensuring that all edges are lined up and pin.

Now sew down each side of the bracelet.

Step 4: - Add the Required Hardware

Add a crimp at every end of the bracelet. With the help of the pliers flatten the crimps.

Slowly pull on the crimps to ensure they're properly attached.

With the pliers, pull open the jump rings enough to fit into the ends of the crimps.

Slide a lobster clasp onto one of the rings and close the ring with the help of the pliers.

Sake Puppets Tips and Diagrams

An embroiderer inspired by her visit to Japan started Sake Puppets to sell her Sashiko-inspired wares. Sake Puppets features a simple, but effective tutorial for Sashiko.

How to Sashiko

Materials Needed:

- patterns
- chalk pencil or transfer paper & tracing tools
- Sashiko needle
- Sashiko thread or embroidery floss
- solid cotton fabric for stitching

Begin by drawing your design onto fabric or transfer a pattern using chalk paper and a tracing tool.

For transferring patterns I recommend using chalk paper and a tracing tool, but you may also use tailor's carbon transfer paper, tissue paper and transfer pens, or the light box method.

For those using chalk or carbon paper, begin by securing your fabric to a tabletop with washi tape or weights. Place the chalk paper on top of the fabric, chalk-side down. Place the pattern on top of the chalk paper. If you need to extend your pattern, make additional copies and tape them together. Once you are satisfied with your arrangement, tape or weight the pattern so it does not move while tracing.

With a tracing tool or pointy object, trace over all of the pattern lines. If desired, you can place a sheet of clear plastic on top of your pattern to help ease the tool along the lines, but it isn't necessary.

When all of the pattern lines have been transferred, you are ready to stitch.

Cut a length of Sashiko yarn and thread your needle. For bold stitches double the yarn, for smaller details and a dainty line, use a single thread. Knot the end.

The pattern has been marked onto the "right" side of your fabric, so you will stitch right over the top of the chalk lines. Pull your needle through the fabric at the start of your first marked line and allow the knot to rest neatly on the back, or "wrong" side.

Leave 1/8" (3 mm) of yarn between the knot and your first stitch—this allows for some "give" when stitching and will help prevent your fabric from puckering.

Work your needle from right to left (or left to right if you're left- handed) along the marked line, making consistent 1/8" to 1/4" (3-5 mm) stitches. Work several stitches onto your needle, then pull your yarn through the fabric. Pull the yarn taught but not tight. Try not to let your fabric pucker. Your stitches should look similar to a running stitch, although slightly longer than the spaces between them. The stitch-to-space ratio for Sashiko is 3:2, but no one is counting, just do your best!

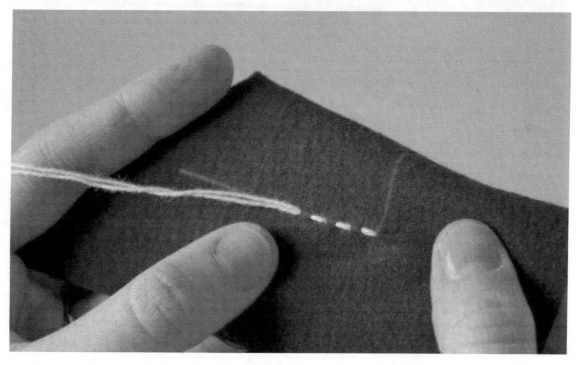

If you notice your fabric is puckering, then your stitches are too tight. To fix this pinch the fabric between your thumb and index finger and run them along your line of stitches to smooth the fabric. Try holding the knotted end steady with one hand while you smooth with the other.

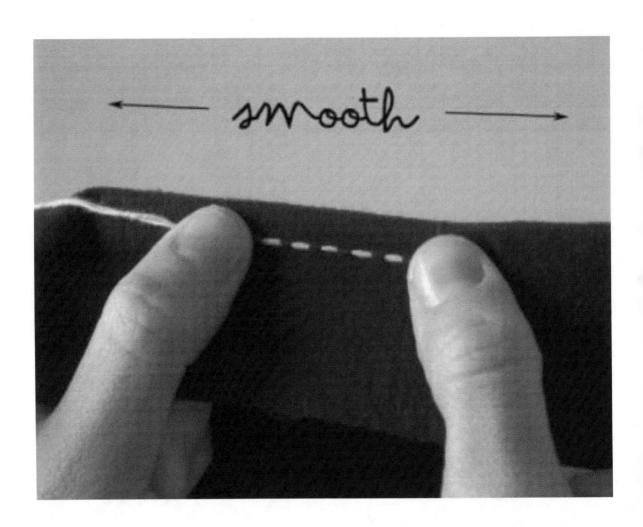

Continue stitching the length of your marked line, smoothing as necessary. When you reach the end of a line, make a small knot on the backside of your fabric and trim any excess yarn. Remember, the chalk-marked side of your fabric is the "right" side, and should be facing you.

Leave a little extra yarn before you tie off your row of stitches with a knot. This allows for some "give" in the case that your fabric shrinks a bit during washing, or you discover later that some of your stitches in that row were too tight.

When turning a corner, leave an extra 1/8" to 1/4" (3-5 mm) of yarn looped on the wrong side of the fabric, again, to help prevent puckering.

Try to keep your corner stitches close together.

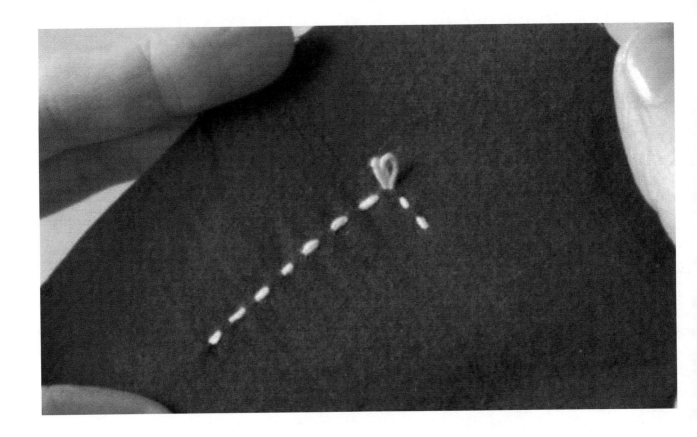

Sashiko Embroidery and Quilting Pattern

This traditional Sashiko pattern comes with 3-dimensional cubes. A good example where this pattern places a vital role is in the production of the Sashiko kitchen towel project.

MOYOZASHI PATTERNS (SASHIKO)

Moyozashi Pattern is one of the basic Sashiko "styles".

Moyozashi uses continuous lines of stitches to make larger patterns, but ensure the lines don't meet.

The fabric thread can't be counted but, the number of stitches may be counted. These are geometric patterns that are repeated on a grid/stitches that never touches or crosses-over.

This class focuses on the Sashiko pattern where the patterns change direction to make a larger one. They are characterized by a series of the dashed lines where running stitches never touch each other.

Moyozashi Patterns comes with repeating geometric shapes comprising straight, curved, and zigzag lines, majorly drawn with a grid as a guide and determination of scale. The dimensions of the grid can vary depending on the pattern and can be adjusted to alter the whole size and scale of the design.

The below are picture demonstrations of Moyozashi Sashiko on indigo dyed linen from a drawn grid and Moyozashi Sashiko on an indigo-dyed hankie from a template.

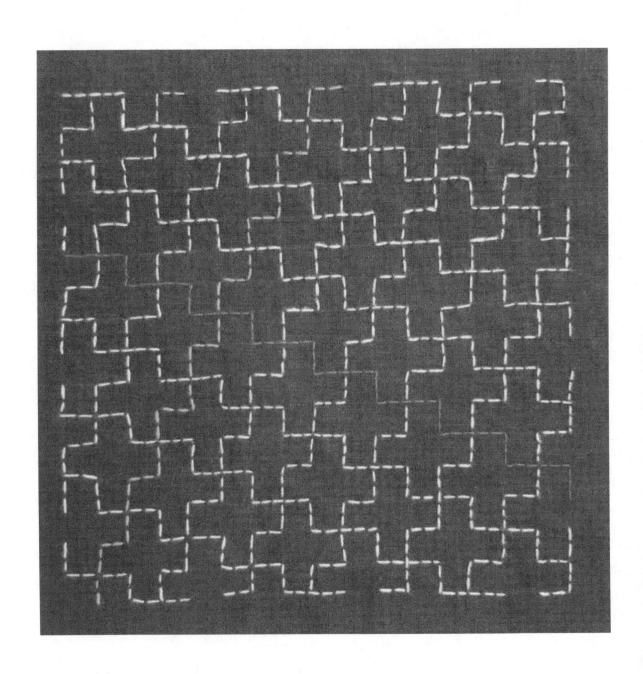

MOTIFS PATTERNS (SASHIKO)

These are designs to be used alone or repeated (family crests, leaves, flowers, kanji characters).

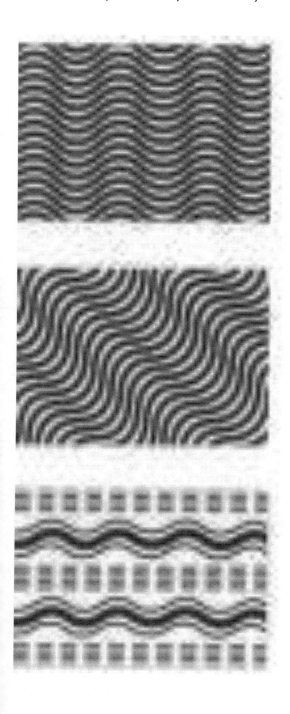
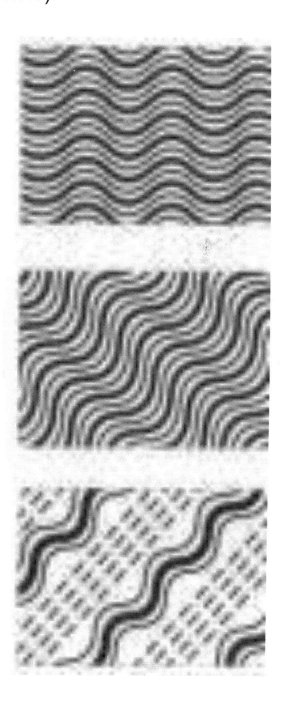

To be specific, a motif is the most primary unit from where a design is created. Its development is possible through a combination of different geometric shapes. Motifs are repeated in various forms to create a pattern whereas patterns are repeated to create various designs. Most traditional motifs are greatly inspired by nature.

In another dimension, the motif is a word which is commonly applied in creative fields such as visual arts, literature, pattern, and design. The term illustrates an important idea that is emphasized in a creative piece through consistent repetition.

The display of a motif could be obvious, such as in a series of paintings that all portray a common theme, for instance farming communities. Most often, a motif will form a gentle basis for the work of which it is a part; in this instance, the motif is usually a vital concept that the artist or designer feels is important and wishes to represent through the immediate sensory experiences brought by the piece.

In the fields of interior design and landscaping, motifs often have a practical application. Instead of representing a critical idea, as in the artistic point of view, the use of the motif in these aspects can sometimes demonstrate a common set of elements that brings up a particular emotional response. For instance, arranging furniture in certain ways can alternatively create feelings of space or intimacy; similarly, a motif can be intended to make visitors feel great excitement.

HITOMEZASHI PATTERNS (ONE STITCH SASHIKO)

Reminiscent of darning patterns/stitches can be woven or cross-over. This pattern comprises of only a series of vertical and horizontal lines that may or may not meet to form bordered shapes. Curves have no part to play in these patterns, however diagonal can.

The easiest form of rows of running stitch was often applied for repairs in garments. If you look back at Moyozashi Pattern, you will find out that threads often intersect and cross each other as part of the design. Although, these designs are more densely stitched than Moyozashi patterns.

Below are picture demonstrations of Hitomezashi Sashiko stitching on indigo dyed linen from a drawn grid and Hitomezashi Sashiko on an indigo cotton hankie from a drawn grid.

These two types of patterns can be combined in a single piece of work to achieve great results. After the combination, the resulting pattern is a spider web Sashiko pattern on the indigo-dyed hankie. See the picture below.

Conclusion

Sashiko is the traditional way of hand stitching and is still popular throughout Japan. There are many different types of Sashiko that have unique patterns, colors, and stitching techniques. The only thing that all Sashiko share is their traditional shape. Traditional Sashiko designs were greatly inspired by nature, such as waves, flowers, troubling waters, clouds, and leaves. The designs are very geometric in nature involving interlocking stars, lines, squares, rectangles, triangles, and circles. Every pattern generally has a history linked to it and comes with peculiar meaning or popular uses.

In the Pattern Library, there are a whole lot of patterns to assist you to execute your various Sashiko projects. There are a lot of patterns in the pattern library that may fall under Moyozashi, Motif, or Hitomezashi patterns respectively.

I hope you have enjoyed these step-by-step instructions and found them easy to follow. There is a lot of information packed into these three pages and I had to leave out many other details, but hopefully you will be able to make your own beautiful Sashiko.

Made in the USA
Middletown, DE
30 September 2023

39828403R00126